Change Leadership
A U.S. Metal Building Industry Perspective

GEORGE W. RIDEOUT, D.B.A.

Dedication

This study is dedicated to my wife, Willie, who has always believed in me. Without her love, support, and understanding, through the good times and bad, this journey would not have been possible. For this, I am forever grateful.

I would like to also recognize my mother, Linda Rideout. Mom, you raised me to be a dreamer; to never give up, and believe that anything is possible. Achieving this goal is testament to this belief system. Thank you for giving me this gift.

Acknowledgments

I have always believed in the expression, "No man is an island." Without a strong support system, a man's accomplishments will be limited. The support system evident throughout this doctoral journey begins with my mentor, Dr. Jane Lillestol. Without her constant "I believe in your ability" attitude, perhaps my spirit would have been wounded and I would not have reached the finish line. Everyone, no matter how driven needs words of encouragement at times, and Dr. Lillestol provided the support umbrella I needed at a professional level to achieve this lofty goal. I cannot express enough my appreciation for all you have done for me. You have left a permanent impression on my life.

I would like to acknowledge my committee members, Dr. Janice Terrell and Dr. James Ziegler, who painstakingly reviewed my work and offered insightful and constructive suggestions. Thank you for going beyond the call of duty to help me finish the journey. I would like to thank my talented editor, Mary Ellen Carew, for helping transform me into a better and more succinct writer. Thank you, Mary Ellen, for pulling me across the reference hurdle. I also want to extend my appreciation to the pilot study and Delphi panel members. Without your willingness to share insight and commitment to participate, this valuable study could not have been completed. Thank you. You know who you are!

Finally, I would like to acknowledge an early mentor, Dr. John Joseph, who encouraged me at a critical stage in my life and believed in my ideas. Dr. Joseph profoundly impacted my thinking as a young college student, and this thinking has guided my life journey thus far. I do not think I would be here today were it not for his early words of encouragement and belief in my ability. Dr. Joseph, you gave me confidence, and for this I am eternally grateful.

Contents

Change Leadership
A U.S. Metal Building Industry Perspective

1 Overview

The twenty-first century has presented new challenges for organizations. Today's business environment, full of economic chaos, demands that businesses change quickly to survive. Research suggests 70% of organizational change initiatives fail, and that major change influences organizational decision-making several times a year (Mueller, 2009; Pellettiere, 2006). Forces such as competitive economic globalization, the green movement, the operating environment, and technology are causing industry and organizational leaders to cope with change. How organizational leaders manage these forces and the inherent change could create a competitive advantage for their organizations (Charan, 2009). Cohen (2008) described a competitive advantage as that which an organization does better than its competitors. Senge (2006) stated learning faster than competitors could be the only competitive advantage available to organizations. Identifying and creating strategies to manage change is integral to organizational learning.

Proactive organizational leaders will use the economic downturn in the early twenty-first century to shed old policies and create new strategies to deal with the rapid pace of change (McGrath & MacMillan, 2009). Employees in organizations with a history of success are more resistant to change than are employees in less successful organizations (McGrath & MacMillan, 2009). That resistance may fuel future challenges and adversely affect competitive advantages (McGrath & MacMillan, 2009). Resistance to change heightens the need for the creation of internal strategies to plan actively for and manage anticipated change rather than simply respond to external pressure created by change.

The purpose of this descriptive qualitative study has been to understand how organizational leaders in the U.S. metal building industry identify and manage the need for change. A review of literature reveals rich information on change management and relevant theory, but none on change management strategies in the U.S. metal building industry. This study may benefit the U.S. metal building industry by increasing the depth of change management knowledge in the industry or filling the knowledge gap, creating efficiency in operations and a competitive advantage in the marketplace. The questionnaire research design used the Delphi method for gathering data from a panel of seven organizational leaders in the U.S. metal building industry.

Background of the Problem

According to Arora (2003), change initiatives fail to produce wanted results 70% of the time. The failure rate espouses the lack of organizational leaders' understanding about how to implement change successfully in the organization. Arora (2003) created theory zyx and argues that three dimensions exist in the change management process: (a) Z-axis or planning, (b) Y-axis or execution, and (c) X-axis or people. The planning axis accounts for organizational leaders creating a vision and long-term strategy. The execution axis entails preparing the organization to accept the change initiative through training and knowledge management. The people axis cements the change initiatives by earning employee trust and reinforcing the need to change. According to Arora (2003), planning, execution, and people account for 99% of change management success.

Walters, Halliday, and Glaser (2002) identified a new business model that could help organizational leaders in the creation of a competitive advantage through market flexibility and key partnerships. The model directs organizational leaders to recognize that change is occurring more often and becoming less predictable. How organizational leaders and their employees respond and whether they embrace change is crucial to future success.

Organizational leaders who refuse to recognize the need to change can cause their organizations to fail. Service Merchandise Corporation, a staple in American business for nearly a century, failed because the company's leaders did not make changes needed to address mounting losses caused by high employee turnover (Phillips, 2005).

Research studies suggest the cost of turnover for Service Merchandise

was $180 million annually (Phillips, 2005). According to Phillips

(2005), Service Merchandise leaders eventually accepted the need to

change and revamped their business model, but the efforts were too

little too late; the company entered bankruptcy.

Arora (2003) argued that organizational change meets

resistance because of human nature's tendency to follow the status quo.

Strong organizational leaders introduce and implement change, whereas

nonleaders, as the general worker populace, strive to meet the status

quo (Arora, 2003). Strong organizational leaders are visionary.

Visionary leaders are deductive thinkers who can create strategies to

lead organizational change to the envisioned result. Inductive thinkers

are managers who have a limited viewpoint beyond their everyday tasks

(Arora, 2003).

Failure of change management strategies often results from a

lack of macro and micro viewpoints by organizational leaders

(Tuominen, 2000). Many leaders lack the ability to link departmental

goals and external influences with organizational goals. Understanding

how internal and external forces influence the organization can help

achieve organizational change success (Tuominen, 2000). Tuominen

(2000) described successful organizational leadership as holistic and created a model for holistic management. The model suggests a top-to-bottom approach linking strategic management, product management, process management, and development management in the organization. The model stresses the need for leaders to recognize the interdependency of all organizational parts including those outside the organization, such as those in the supply chain.

Newman (2009) described the leader's role in creating high performing organizational culture as promoting organizational strengths to compensate for weak areas or gaps in the organization. The holistic model posed by Newman (2009) confirms the views of Tuominen (2000) that good leadership links the organization's departments and processes. "Customer insight, business alignment, technology, and execution are at the core of building an effective innovation initiative" (Newman, 2009, p. 21).

Change management and using innovation or out-of-the-box thinking to create and drive organizational strategy is a form of holistic management. Organizational change may have a ripple effect; the influence of change can extend beyond the walls of a department or beyond organizational boundaries. McLaughlin (2009) stated that technology-based change initiatives often fail because organizational leaders do not consider the influence change may have on the organization, including nontechnical areas.

Senge (2006) described the learning organization as an entity whose parts are constantly evolving and becoming better. This description by Senge calls for leaders to follow a holistic management model. Senge (2006) created his argument about systems thinking, aptly coined *the fifth discipline*. Senge (2006) stated that effective organizational leaders overcome change resistance by working to reduce the resistance through isolation. The 1940s force-field analysis model developed by Kurt Lewin describes the status quo or the norm in an organization as supporters of change meeting resistance by those who do not support change (Beitler, 2006). Employees' comfort with the norm causes resistance to change and correlates with leadership effectiveness (Senge, 2006).

Tuominen (2000) stated that "leadership brings change" (p. 259). Leaders must lead the charge for change, keep a steady hand on change initiatives, and know when to step aside and let change occur in the organization (Tuominen, 2000). The ability of leaders to identify, manage, and successfully implement change initiatives faster and at a higher success rate than competitors may create an advantage for the organization. A company's leaders' ability to identify opportunities before competitors is a competitive advantage (Tuominen, 2000). Organizational leadership cannot take advantage of this *first-to-market* knowledge without the ability to make the vision reality, requiring a systems approach to change management (Tuominen, 2000).

Researching change policies, including how organizations identify and manage change, may benefit the U.S. metal building industry and industry in general, including the academic community. Organizational leaders may develop new approaches to change management and recognize how managing change correlates with creating a competitive advantage in the marketplace. The research may identify a new change model and areas of study to expand the body of knowledge in change management; this may advance both the corporate and the academic communities.

Problem Statement

How organizational leaders manage change can affect long-term success (Cohen, 2008). Many organizational leaders struggle with the critical thinking and analytical skills necessary to manage change quickly (Fodness, 2005). Internal and external forces can cause an organization to change. Change in the twenty-first century is constant, increasingly difficult to manage, and an important determinant in organizational survival (Arora, 2003; Norbutus, 2007). Christensen (2006) argued change can cause organizations to fail, including organizations admired for their longevity and prior success. To overcome disruptive change forces, organizational leaders should become proactive and learn that sometimes no one right answer may exist; organizational leaders must strive to see clearly and learn to lead with an open mind (Arora, 2003; Christensen, 2006).

Beitler (2006) described a competitive advantage as a leader's ability to maximize organization skills or core competencies to overtake competitors. Managing change is a core competency. The specific problem is that an organization may lose its competitive advantage and fail if the leaders cannot recognize and manage change quickly (McDonald, 2000).

The descriptive qualitative study examined change management strategies used by a population of leaders in the U.S. metal building industry and how these strategies have influenced competitive advantage. The questionnaire research design incorporated the Delphi method and polled a sample population of seven industry executives. A qualitative research study is appropriate for gathering subjective data; a questionnaire design is a form of qualitative research (Borrego, Douglas & Amelink, 2009). The research results were used to support a model for identifying, implementing, and managing change. By analyzing the literature review, the researcher had an opportunity to identify and describe change management strategies, both internal and external to the industry, and to increase the breadth of information examined.

Purpose

The purpose of the descriptive qualitative study was to explore change management methods and strategies used by seven leaders in the U.S. metal building industry. The specific population for the study was leaders in the U.S. metal building industry. Using the questionnaire research design of the Delphi method allowed the researcher to gather data from a sample of seven executives in the population.

The Rand Corporation created the Delphi method in the 1950s for military forecasting (Grisham, 2009; Padel & Midmore, 2005). By using the Delphi method, the researchers gather data on a subjective and complex topic by polling a panel of experts; a central mediator reviews the data for consensus (Grisham, 2009; Padel & Midmore, 2005). Grisham (2009) stated the Delphi method was scientific and researchers could gather insight from the resulting data into areas in which quantitative analysis may fail; using the technique provides researchers with a high degree of forecasting accuracy. Shank (2006) described qualitative research as "a form of systematic empirical inquiry into meaning" (p. 4). Research suggests Delphi is a "reliable empirical method" (Grisham, 2009, p. 116).

The Delphi panel of leaders from seven companies in the U.S. metal building industry (a) had a minimum of 10 years executive level industry experience, and (b) worked for an organization operating for a minimum of 10 years. The researcher in the present study identified candidates from membership in the Metal Building Manufacturer Association (MBMA) and listings from the 2010 Metal Directory and Resource Guide, published by Metal Construction News (MCN). The researcher attempted to identify two executives in each qualified organization who met the experience criteria, thus creating two lists. Leaders from up to 141 organizations in the U.S. metal building industry received invitations to take part in the study (see Appendix A for a list of potential organizations, and Appendix B for the individual request for participation).

The invitation process took place in four rounds, beginning with the first list of qualified executives. If contacting this list was unsuccessful, then the researcher sent out new invitations to the second list of qualified executives. The rounds continued until the researcher attained the goal of seven qualified executives. Once the selection process was complete, the researcher began the data gathering. The researcher used the data gathered as support for a model based on the study research questions that industry leaders could use to forecast, implement, and manage future change to create competitive advantage.

Significance of the Study

This descriptive qualitative study can help organizational leaders in the U.S. metal building industry identify why and how change occurs, create strategies to manage change internally and externally, and create a competitive advantage for their organizations. The present study provides a comparison of change methods, allowing organizational leaders and the academic community to develop new ideas about change practices and leadership strategies that may be outside the scope of ordinary consideration. The research also provided insight into markets that organizational leaders have considered exploring for future growth.

The study served as a basis for using the gathered information to support a model that industry leaders could use to manage change initiatives in their organizations. The model, based on study research questions, provides a template to the metal building industry for creating a competitive advantage by managing change. The model also serves the academic community and leadership field by adding to the depth of knowledge regarding change management strategies.

Nature of the Study

The qualitative method allowed researchers to gather subjective data that is descriptive, although not necessarily statistically significant (Borrego, Douglas & Amelink, 2009). Salkind (2003) identified ways to gather qualitative data including interviews, case studies, and historical data. Quantitative research identified associations between outcomes and variables (Borrego, Douglas & Amelink, 2009). Researchers were able to identify independent and dependent variables and gather statistically relevant data (Borrego, Douglas & Amelink, 2009). Because of the descriptive and subjective nature of the study, the qualitative method was the best option for gathering the information from the research participants.

The research study used a population of executives in the U.S. metal building industry. The Delphi method was used to poll the population to gather data. The results were used to support a change model to benefit various industries, including the academic community. The qualitative method provided a way to gather data that is difficult to identify quantitatively. For instance, an individual organizational leader's approach may have benefitted many organizations, but because the approach was internal, other organizations might never have become aware of the processes implemented to achieve success. The qualitative method provided a way to harness this data.

The Delphi method was proper for gathering data on topics that were subjective and difficult to analyze using traditional techniques (Grisham, 2009). Delphi benefits included the following:

1. Opportunity to gather unbiased data from anonymous experts in a field—each panel member did not know the identity of other panel members; and

2. Research suggested high accuracy rates when the group reached a consensus (Grisham, 2009).

Knab (2008) used a qualitative approach to study success factors when entering emerging markets. The qualitative method and Delphi research design allowed Knab (2008) to approach a subjective area and isolate relevant data to form a consensus. Similar to the Knab (2008) study, this change management study was used to analyze subjective data, soliciting views from a population selected because of expertise in the U.S. metal building industry.

The study required gathering subjective data that could vary by organization. Understanding how to use the Delphi method effectively influenced study results. Newstrom and Davis (2002) identified requirements to ensure a successful Delphi-based study: time to gather and analyze data, finding the right experts, communication, and the need for panel experts to engage in the study.

Thematic analysis was the basis for data interpretation. Shank (2006) described thematic analysis as identifying themes or patterns in the gathered data. Analysis of the data gathered from the Delphi panel

13

identified a consensus or common theme. Once a consensus was found among the panel, conclusions from the data formed the support for a new change management model.

Research Questions

The purpose of this current research study was to explore the change management strategies of seven organizational leaders in the U.S. metal building industry. The intent was to identify how change management strategies may have translated into a competitive advantage for an organization. The study used the Delphi method to gather data from a panel of experts in the U.S. metal building industry.

The research questions for the study correlated with change management strategies and helped create conclusions that could add to the body of knowledge available to the U.S. metal building industry and the academic community. The central question providing the foundation for the study was: How do leaders in the U.S. metal building industry identify, manage, and translate change management into a competitive advantage for their organizations? The four related sub-questions were as follows:

1. How do leaders in the U.S. metal building industry perceive change management and identify, recognize, and differentiate between internal and external change forces?

2. How do leaders in the U.S. metal building industry respond to internal and external change, and how do these forces affect their change management strategies?

3. How do leaders in the U.S. metal building industry define competitive advantage, and how does change management influence creating a competitive advantage?

4. How do responses of leaders in the U.S. metal building industry reflect systems thinking, and what theories outlined in the conceptual or theoretical framework do their responses support?

Conceptual or Theoretical Framework

Research shows humans have studied the future since Sumerian days almost 6,000 years ago (Joseph, 2007). The field of social science and the study of change management and organizational change (OC) have evolved and have been important topics critical to organizational strategy and competitive success. As the world continues to become increasingly interdependent and traditional organizational hierarchies less significant, the OC field will become critical for organizational success and, more important, preserving a sustainable competitive advantage (Senge, 2006).

The research study drew support from many theories and models including work by Kurt Lewin, considered the father of social science. Lewin's work influenced the ideology of change management and set the standard for the OC field today (Coghlan & Brannick, 2003). Lewin's work provided a solid foundation and supported systems theory, the theory that underpinned the research study. Other theories that further supported the research were chaos theory, disruptive change theory, futurology, holistic management, intentional change theory, and resource-based theory.

Systems Theory

Systems theory was the basis for the theoretical framework that underpinned this study. Information was rich on systems theory, coming from a diverse group ranging from scientists to organizational consultants. The father of systems theory was German biologist Ludwig von Bertalanffy (Mulej et al., 2004).

Bertalanffy created the idea of general systems theory (GST) during a time when the world was in chaos and people saw the implications of Hitler and Mussolini; the actions of a few influenced millions worldwide (Mulej et al., 2004). Bertalanffy hoped GST would show the world's interconnectedness and break down the walls of specialization (Mulej et al., 2004). The GST, although widely disputed for being unrealistic with little hard evidence supporting the Bertalanffy posits, provided the foundation for systems thinking today (Mulej et al., 2004). The GST also helped support what Bertalanffy was trying to stray from, the specialization of systems thinking. Bertalanffy's ideas spawned subsequent work by theorists including Deming, Ackoff, and Senge, who each parlayed the GST into a specialty construct. The focus on these individual specialties supported the view that all parts of an organization were interdependent and individually could influence the organizational structure and efficiency.

Chaos Theory

Chaos theory had roots in systems thinking but extended the systems approach to recognize that change was unpredictable (Bussolari & Goodell, 2009). The ideology of chaos theory began with the early work of Henri Poincare whose experiments showed the simplest systems could create complex, unpredictable, and chaotic behavior (Bussolari & Goodell, 2009). The butterfly effect underpinned chaos theory and helped lay the groundwork for today's use of theory when applied to organizations: small changes influenced future results (Bussolari & Goodell, 2009). The butterfly effect also helped explain the relationship "between small, seemingly innocuous events and large catastrophic results" (Burlando, 1994, p. 57). Because change was constant (Oosten, 2006), even small changes over time could have significant influence on organizational performance. Perhaps Greek philosopher Heraclitus said it best when he stated "nothing endures but change" (Mueller, 2009, p. 70).

Disruptive Change Theory

Christensen created a theory based on disruptive innovation: the disruptive change theory (Christensen & Mangelsdorf, 2009). Christensen (2005) explained how the rapid evolution of technology could cause disruptive change in organizations. Christensen (2005) stated that organizational leaders who could aptly predict disruptive change caused by technology could improve their decision-making ability.

Futurology

McLean (2007) described futurology as using knowledge gained from historical or past events to shape future strategy. Research suggests futurism studies have dated back 6,000 years to the Sumerian days, but the ideology of futurism did not take hold until the twentieth century. Well-known futurists have included Aristotle, Frances Bacon, Voltaire, and Bertalanffy, considered the father of systems theory (Joseph, 2007).

Holistic Management

Knowledge, how organizational leaders used collective intellectual capital, and how actively leaders pursued new knowledge created a sustainable advantage for their organizations (Vorakulpipat & Rezgui, 2008). The critical word was *collective*. How leaders integrated the organization internally and externally to take advantage of knowledge throughout the collective system have defined future success. Webster's Dictionary defines holism as "a theory or belief emphasizing the importance of the whole and the interdependence of its parts" ("Anonymous," 1996, p. 330). This ideology formed the basis for organizational holistic management's recognizing that all business functions internal and external have influenced each other.

Intentional Change Theory

Intentional change theory, also known as "self-directed learning," had roots in human behavior and how humans created long-term change in their lives (Boyatzis, 2006, p. 609; Oosten, 2006). Boyatzis (2006) was an early pioneer of intentional change studies. Intentional change theory was "a complex system," a system that was a culmination of other systems and could act independently of the individual parts (Boyatzis, 2006, p. 608). For instance, complex systems existed in many organizations, in which departments operated independently or together to form a complex system or network.

Resource-based Theory

Resource-based theory (RBT) had roots in the relationship between organizational leadership, employee management, and competitive advantage (Yang, 2009). Research suggested competitive advantage was a result of internal and external forces (Yang, 2009). Organizational leaders who managed the influence of these forces and the resulting change gained organizational market advantage (Yang, 2009). Resource-based theory was integral to the latter construct. For instance, how an organization's leaders managed key resources, such as employees, influenced efficiency and the organization's competitive status in the marketplace.

Definitions

The purpose of the following review of definitions is to ensure consistency in the research and to avoid discrepancy between the author's and readers' interpretation.

- **Competitive advantage**. Tuominen (2000) described a competitive advantage as anything an organization might do to its products and services to distinguish the organization from the competition. Dengler (2006) citing Jack Welch former Chief Executive Officer (CEO) of General Electric (GE) stated that a competitive advantage rested in an organization's ability to learn quickly and translate that learning into strategy.

- **Delphi method.** The Delphi method uses an expert panel to forecast and deal with a complex but subjective topic (Gabb et al., 2006; Grisham, 2008). Questionnaires are used to gather data; analysis involves looking for common themes in panel responses. Once the researcher has determined consensus, the researcher may draw conclusions. The method has roots in military forecasting but has spawned a multidisciplinary research design to explore varied issues. Research suggests the Delphi method might increase creativity in the decision-making process and be accurate (Gabb et al., 2006; Grisham, 2008).

- **Executive.** An executive is an organizational leader responsible for implementing policy (Anonymous, 1996). For this research, an executive has been any organizational leader considered a senior decision-maker.

- **Expert.** This research followed a multipronged definition of the term *expert.* An expert was (a) a stakeholder, (b) someone who had firsthand professional knowledge of the subject, or (c) a person who gathered and analyzed data from other experts (Gabb et al., 2006).

- **Organizational change.** Many definitions exist for organizational change. For this study, organizational change encompasses how an organization transformed over time. Lönnqvist, Kianto and Sillanpaa (2009) stated organizational change was obvious by watching the transformation process; change could be found "by comparing the organization before and after the transformation" (p. 561).

- **Systems theory.** Ludwig von Bertalanffy created general systems theory (GST) (Mulej et al., 2004). A system is a group of highly interconnected parts that can create its own behavior (Meadows, 2008). Systems are everywhere, from the human body to the multinational corporation, with many organizational levels and departments.

Assumptions

This research followed assumptions about the U.S. metal building industry and change management. The first assumption was that organizational leaders in the U.S. metal building industry are constantly seeking opportunities to increase competitive advantage for their organizations. Another important assumption was that industry leaders have the desire and see the value in change management. A third assumption was that organizational leaders in the U.S. metal building industry have change management strategies in place. Finally, the researcher has worked in the U.S. metal building industry for nearly 16 years in sales and management. The effect of, and response to, both internal and external forces in the industry motivated the researcher to study this subject and validate or disprove any related preconceived assumptions.

Scope

The scope of the study included seven executives in the U.S. metal building industry. The executives worked for different organizations, and their geographical locations varied across the United States. Each executive participating in the study met the following criteria: (a) had a minimum of 10 years executive level industry experience, and (b) worked for an organization operating for a minimum of 10 years. The executives received a 13-part round one questionnaire (see Appendix C) asking questions about change management techniques and the relationship of change management to competitive strategy.

Limitations

The research study was subject to limitations. For instance, the study used data gathered from seven U.S. metal building industry executives. The viewpoints of these executives might not accurately represent the entire U.S. metal building industry, and study results can only reflect the viewpoints of this seven-member Delphi panel. Powell (2003) stated that although studies should seek to include as many participants as possible, empirical data do not support any given Delphi panel size for accuracy. A second limitation was in the selection of the executive panel. The metal building industry is made up of many privately owned organizations who might not reveal data, therefore, making the qualifying of executives difficult. This also limits the availability of participants because executives who may add significantly to study results may not have received an invitation. A third limitation was the sample size available for study. According to the Metal Building Manufacturer's Association (MBMA) and the 2010 Metal Directory and Resource Guide, 141 metal building manufacturers are in the United States (see Appendix A for a list of potential organizations). Of the 141 organizations identified, a much smaller number met the time in business criteria and had executives who qualified for study invitation. The study also could suffer from a panel member's deciding not to complete the study.

The researcher works in the metal building industry and has significant experience in sales and middle management. The researcher's experience should not have produced research bias because the study focused on gathering data from senior level executives only. The researcher excluded his employer, and any companies or leaders with whom the researcher has existing or prior relationships from study participation in order to further limit research bias.

The Delphi technique requires rounds of questionnaires and thematic analysis to identify consensus among panel participants. The thematic analysis might be subject to research bias because the researcher is the interpreter of study results. To limit this potential bias, the researcher posited that study offered consensus only when convergence of data was obvious. The researcher also offered a definition of consensus to further support research findings. The Delphi method could have hindered statistical limitations because the design does "not call for expert panels to be representative samples for statistical purposes" (Powell, 2003, p. 378).

Delimitations

The current research study was limited to executives working in the U.S. metal building industry. All panel members met the following: (a) had a minimum of 10 years executive level industry experience, and (b) worked for an organization operating for a minimum of 10 years. The executives participated anonymously, meaning no panel member knew who the other members were. Executives received questionnaires via the Internet. Thematic analysis provided the foundation for data analysis. The focus was on identification of themes from the data and areas of consensus among the panel members.

Summary

An understanding of change management and how organizational leaders ready themselves and identify future change may lead to the creation of a sustainable competitive advantage. The ability to change faster than competitors is a critical part of organizational survival (Dengler, 2006). Organizations risk losing their competitive

advantage and may fail if organizational leaders cannot grasp and

manage change (Dengler, 2006; McDonald, 2000).

The current descriptive research study was used to try to

bridge the gap between how leaders identify change and how they carry

out strategies to take advantage of this knowledge. Organizational

culture and learning are important ingredients to effective

organizational change management. Morabito, Sack, Stohr, and Bhate

(2009) stated that organizational culture influences learning; learning is

integral to change occurring in the organization. A resistance to change

caused by organizational culture stymies learning and prevents change

(Morabito et al., 2009). Lewin's force-field model supports this

ideology of leadership working to reduce resistance.

It behooves organizational leaders to recognize what causes

change and how to translate this knowledge into quantifiable strategies

their organizations can use to create competitive advantage. The

purpose of this study was to identify how organizational leaders use

change management to create a competitive advantage in the

marketplace. The general study focus was on the U.S. metal building

industry and how seven industry leaders managed change. How these

leaders identified or forecasted change, implemented change policies,

and used change to help their respective organizations gain a competitive advantage were key research points. Although the study focus was narrow, the research implications were broad and positively influenced other industries and the academic community. The research data also provided support for a new change management model.

Chapter one outlined the background, purpose, theory, and why the research study might serve U.S. metal building industry leaders, industry in general, and the academic community. The study added to the body of knowledge in the field of change management and, more important, filled the change management knowledge gap that exists in the U.S. metal building industry. Chapter two provides a review of the literature and digs deeper into the theory and literature that support the need for this study.

2 Review of Literature

The current qualitative research study has addressed how organizational leaders in the U.S. metal building industry may use change management to create a competitive advantage. The study used a questionnaire design and gathered data from an expert panel using the Delphi technique. The purpose of the study was to identify the specific methods and change management strategies used by seven leaders in the U.S. metal building industry.

The literature on change management includes important contributions from Arora (2003), Beitler (2006), Christensen (2006), Dalkey and Helmer (1963), Grisham (2009), Joseph (2007), Senge (2006), and others who helped shape the field. Significant data exists on the field of organizational change and strategies to manage change in the organization, including systems and related theories. The influence of change management on competitive advantage appears in the literature beginning in the late twentieth century. No data exists, however, on how leaders in the U.S. metal building industry manage change. The study may fill this knowledge gap.

Chapter two will encompass a literature review of change theories supporting the research focus. The literature review will provide an opportunity to examine data about the research problem, the history of change management and relevant theories, and identify

gaps in the literature. The literature review will support the research

study on how managing change may create a competitive advantage for

organizations. Systems theory will underscore the emphasis, but other

change theories will support the systems ideology. The theories studied

will include a) chaos theory, b) disruptive change theory, c) futurology,

d) holistic management, e) intentional change theory, f) resource-based

theory, and g) systems theory.

Chapter two follows a hierarchal structure that will synergize

the theories supporting the research study. Each theory will receive a

thorough review, including the history and support for the theory, and

how the theory underscores systems theory and change management.

The literature review will include an analysis of competitive advantage

and how innovation through change may promote an organizational

competitive advantage.

Title Searches, Articles, Research Documents, and Journals Researched

Various sources provided data for the literature review

including: (a) University of Phoenix Library, (b) ProQuest, (c)

EBSCOhost, and (d) Gale PowerSearch. Literature search terms

included: (a) forecasting change, (b) change forces, (c) change theory,

(d) organizational readiness, and (e) competitive advantage. The literature review included data from 118 sources; specifically: 88 peer-reviewed journal articles, 27 books, and three dissertations.

Historical Overview

Man has studied change for thousands of years (Joseph, 2007). Theorists such as Pythagoras, Socrates, Plato, Aristotle, Thomas Aquinas, and Voltaire guided early work on future studies and methods humans used to identify and manage change (Joseph, 2007). The twentieth century proved a rich period for organizational change practice and theory development. Demers (2007) identified three stages in organizational change development during the twentieth century:

1. Late 1940s to 1970s—the post-World War II era heralded the idea of organizational adaptation or gradual change, where leaders could choose to adapt their organizations to the changing environment;

2. Late 1970s to 1980—the focus shifted to organizational transformation and change because of rapid or disruptive changes in the environment; and

3. 1990s to present—the learning organization became the emphasis for modern day organizational change theory.

Work by Lewin, Bertalanffy, and the RAND Corporation helped lay the foundation for the stages outlined by Demers (2007). Social psychologist Kurt Lewin, regarded as the father of social science, contributed to the idea of planned change and action research, where leaders involved employees in the change process (Coghlan & Brannick, 2003).

Schenck (2007) commented on man's difficulty to deal with change because of a natural fear of change. Change has roots in creativity requiring people to do something differently, and to move outside the norm of how they operate (Schenk, 2007). This innovative thinking causes leaders to recognize the value of a systems approach to strategic planning and sustainable competitive advantage.

Systems Theory

Ludwig von Bertalanffy, a biologist by trade, developed general systems theory (GST) during the height of World War II (Mulej et al., 2004). GST helped satisfy the need for holistic thinking that became evident during the war (Mulej et al., 2004). Perhaps Bertalanffy himself described the ideology of systems thinking best when he posited:

> Man in the early culture, and even primitives today, experience themselves as being "thrown" into a hostile world, governed by chaotic and incomprehensible demonic forces which, at best, may be propitiated or influenced by way of magical practices. Philosophy and its descendent, science was born when the early Greeks learned to consider or find, in the

experienced world, an order or kosmos which was intelligible and, hence, controllable by thought and rational action. (Von Bertalanffy, 1972, p. 407)

Scientists at the RAND Corporation continued work on GST to include systems analysis. "Ed Paxson, a RAND engineer, came up with the term "*systems analysis*" in 1947" while overseeing "the Evaluation of Military Worth Section" at RAND (Abella, 2008, p. 57). Systems analysis expanded on operational research (OR) that based decisions on known systems and known data (Abella, 2008). The technique allowed researchers to identify unknown systems and answer open-ended questions about which little to no data existed (Abella, 2008). According to Abella (2008), systems analysis was the medium for thinking outside the box. Perhaps this out-of-the-box thinking helped RAND scientists create the Delphi method.

Boulding (1956) supported the Bertalanffy argument that scientific disciplines should stray from specialization, work together to share, and develop knowledge. Knowledge results when people interact in groups; specialization or creating subgroups in disciplines can breakdown knowledge development (Boulding, 1956; Mockler, 1968). Theorists Bertalanffy and Boulding feared a breakdown in communication between scientific disciplines could jeopardize knowledge management and development. Bertalanffy created GST to transcend the lines between scientific disciplines, and to create a mechanism or ideology to share and develop knowledge through communication (Mockler, 1968).

Johnson, Kast, and Rosenzweig (1964), and Mockler (1968) studied GST and applied systems to business management and strategy. Mockler (1968) described a system as a structured set of individual components that worked in tandem to achieve a common goal. The definition by Mockler (1968) confirmed earlier work by Johnson, Kast, and Rosenzweig (1964), who argued that systems thinking created a foundation for leaders to visualize the whole organization as a complex system influenced by the internal and external environment.

Deming and Ackoff expanded the scope of systems thinking. Ackoff described systems "as a collection of interacting parts with a purpose," and proposed that systems became more efficient when all parts worked together (Maccoby, 2010, p. 68-69). Deming, a trained statistician, applied a systems approach to organizational efficiency. Deming helped the Japanese create lean processes, and, in the 1980s, consulted with Ford Motor Company on quality (Maccoby, 2010). Focusing on quality control and organizational efficiency, Deming never lost sight of the systems influence on organizational processes. For instance, Deming believed employees were most productive when happy at work, and the organizational system influenced this happiness (Maccoby, 2010).

Modern day systems theorist Peter Senge coined systems thinking as the fifth discipline organizations should use when creating strategy. Systems' thinking draws together the organization and the remaining four disciplines: individual mastery, "mental models," shared organizational vision, and "team learning" (Senge, 2006, p. 7-9). Without systems' thinking, organizational leadership may not be able to account for the forces that influence and possibly hinder making future visions a reality (Senge, 2006).

Leaders wanting change management success should make sure organizational strategy, skills, and structures align (Carter, 2008). This recommendation by Carter (2008) lends further credence to GST and the comments by Senge (2006), suggesting that, without alignment internally and externally, the organization may fail when trying to carry out and manage change. Knowledge creation (KC) is an extension of this alignment thinking, where all parts of an organization internally and externally work to create knowledge as a complex system. Leonard-Barton (as cited in Chen, 2008) identified four ways organizational leaders may create knowledge:

- Learn from experience—employees will gain knowledge through performing tasks.

- Implement new knowledge—integrating new knowledge
  into the organization requires employee buy-in;

- Trial and error—experimenting may provide opportunities
  to try new processes and harness knowledge; and

- Networking—using external sources to identify
  knowledge.

Drucker (1999), in *Management Challenges for the 21st Century*,
stated that change leaders would use systematic innovation to create
opportunity. This systematic innovation causes organizational leaders
to take a pro-active approach to change management, and scan the
environment for future change regularly. Drucker's (1999) argument
supported the need for harnessing new knowledge; a position
Bertalanffy took more than 50 years earlier, showing the value of
innovation for the twenty-first century and beyond: opportunity.

Chaos Theory

Charles Darwin's theory of evolution was responsible for
creating the intrigue into how organisms react and adapt to predictable
change (Bussolari & Goodell, 2009). Turn-of-the-century scientist
Henri Poincare showed the first linkage to chaos theory by proving that
even noncomplex systems could experience erratic unpredictable
complex behavior (Bussolari & Goodell, 2009). Poincare's thinking
challenged Newtonian ideas and how scientists viewed the universe.

Chaos theory maintained the universe was not predictable, and

challenged thinking that everything happens in an orderly or linear

manner (Kuhfittig & Davis, 1990).

Understanding chaos may give man the ability to understand

how change occurs. Scientists worldwide are studying chaotic behavior

in organic systems. Many consider chaos theory "one of the great

discoveries of the twentieth century with Einstein's theory and

quantum mechanics" (Kuhfittig & Davis, 1990, p. 8). According to

Kuhfittig and Davis (1990), chaos theory finds legitimacy in four

principles:

- Change is non-linear—this defies historical thinking that
  everything in world happens in an orderly fashion;

- Small changes influence long-term outcomes;

- Chaotic patterns occur continuously and repeat
  themselves, forming complex systems; and

- Understanding how to identify future chaotic change
  appears impossible.

Edward Lorenz, a MIT meteorologist in the 1960s, helped

solidify the idea of chaos theory while studying models he created to

forecast weather (Bussolari & Goodell, 2009; Resnicow & Page, 2008).

Lorenz recognized small decimal point changes in his weather

calculations could change the output significantly, and create complex, unpredictable results (Kuhfittig & Davis, 1990). Lorenz coined the term "the butterfly effect" from the data pattern created during his simulation. The butterfly effect supported Poincare's idea that even small changes over time could affect a system (Bussolari & Goodell, 2009). More important, Lorenz's work helped jump start chaos theory studies because the butterfly effect showed patterns in the chaos. Since Lorenz, scientists have applied chaos theory to countless applications including stock market interpretation, how smoke rises from a cigarette, and identifiable patterns in the way water randomly drips from a faucet (Kuhfittig & Davis, 1990).

Chaos theory is similar to the idea of complex adaptive systems (CAS). Alaa (2009) described CAS as systems that constantly change independently and in response to internal and external forces; organizations adapt unpredictably to changing conditions. Karp (2006) stated, "Organizations are complex systems" (p. 4). Leaders who can manage their businesses on the fringes of chaos may reach unforeseen levels of innovation and allow the business to change constantly to meet environmental demands (Stanley, 1999).

Resnicow and Page (2008) identified three components of chaotic change: (a) change is usually dramatic; (b) change happens quickly, making the change hard to foresee; and (c) change often influences many areas in an organization. The stock market shows the ideology behind chaos theory. For instance, prices move in unpredictable ways because individual investors follow unique strategies, but sometimes chaos results and the market moves in unison. Resnicow and Page (2008) described this behavior as a tipping point, where chaotic change happens abruptly and is difficult to predict, but the effects are controllable through trading rules and regulations. A similar thought process may be found in organizations and the influence internal and external forces have on the behavior of employees. Organizational leaders must continually become better, evolve, and decide quickly to keep a competitive advantage and, more important, to keep up with quickly changing environmental conditions (Alaa, 2009; Tsai & Yen, 2008).

Organizational leaders may create a competitive advantage by using CAS ideas (Stanley, 1999). To do so requires leaders to understand the causes of change, and not limit their thinking to one idea or concept (Karp, 2006). Karp (2006) described three areas leaders should consider about organizational change:

- Organizations consist of complex networks that link people and influence the organization;

- People do not act or behave in rational ways; rather people will behave unpredictably; and

- The internal and external environment is dynamic, causing organizations to behave unpredictably and become hard to micromanage; leaders must identify nontraditional ways to manage their organizations.

Too often leaders rely on solutions that caused their organizations to succeed in the past. These ideas by Karp (2006) confirm that leaders can no longer rely on old methods of solving problems but rather must identify new methods to handle the unpredictable. Most organizational systems try to uphold the norm or the status quo (Karp, 2006). Future success depends on leaders challenging the norm. Social scientist Kurt Lewin created force-field analysis to explain how organizations react to change. The technique describes supporting forces working against resisting forces to create the status quo in the organization (Beitler, 2006). Reducing resistance to change may help leaders carry out new ideas and help their organizations move forward.

Chaos theory supports systems theory because the theory helps explain how complex systems adapt to and influence the environment. Gonnering (2010) said leaders continue to run their organizations like "simple, linear, equilibrium-seeking, and isolated systems" (p. 7). Systems are chaotic and behave in a nonlinear fashion, influencing other systems and creating a complex network of interacting systems (Gonnering, 2010). Leaders who recognize the chaotic behavior of their organizations and systems may find opportunity in the chaos (Charan, 2009).

Disruptive Change Theory

Christensen created the disruptive innovation theory to help explain how organizations that create technological innovation can displace those who do not (Christensen & Mangelsdorf, 2009). The disruptive innovation theory proposes that leaders who recognize forerunners to disruptive change help their organizations gain an advantage in the marketplace (Anthony & Christensen, 2005). Identifying the next threat is a challenge leader's face in the new global economy, where smaller more innovative competitors are on the horizon.

Companies typically innovate faster than their customers can adapt, often creating overpriced products that meet the needs of only a few consumers because of a narrow focus on profit rather than value (Anthony & Christensen, 2005). Less perceptive consumers who may have interest in the product but cannot afford the high price become disenfranchised, and more important, the product bypasses new consumers. This leaves room for more nimble value-seeking competitors, who can use disruptive innovation to meet the needs of the less-knowledgeable and new consumer and earn market share from their larger counterparts.

Hwang and Christensen (2008) described two forms of innovation: a) sustainable and b) disruptive. Sustainable refers to long established products refined over time to meet customer demands, and disruptive to new, scaled down products designed to offer economical alternatives to existing products. Eventually, because of lower cost and high quality, the newer products catch on with the customer base and become in demand, eventually moving the disruptive innovation into the sustainable innovation category. Established organizations are usually successful when warding off new competitors hoping to gain market share of products and services considered sustaining innovations, but they lose the battle when faced with disruptive innovations (Anthony & Christensen, 2005).

Although Christensen created the disruptive change theory because of technological innovation, the theory may apply to other fields influenced by innovation. For instance, many consider the twenty-first century financial debacle on Wall Street and the health care crisis as precipitated by innovation (Christensen & Mangelsdorf, 2009). Hwang and Christensen (2008) argued that disruptive innovation could positively affect business and create opportunity. New, smaller firms seeking market share are notorious for using disruptive measures based on innovation to earn market share from more established firms. Well-known users of disruptive innovation to gain market share include

Toyota and Canon, whose leaders used economical models to gain market share from giants such as General Motors and Xerox (Hwang & Christensen, 2008). Toyota and Canon are organizations that illustrate how new entrants to an established market can create market share by innovating existing products.

Disruptive innovation causes leaders to reexamine constantly how the organization foresees coming change, and new, smaller competitors on the horizon who may be more nimble and more focused on customer needs and value. Norton and Pine (2009) expanded on this by stating that most companies used incremental innovation to modify their products to meet the needs of new customers through functionality rather than need. The changes usually meet only the needs of a few customers, causing competitors to step in and take market share through disruptive innovation. "As this happens, whole markets can shift as emerging businesses become the leaders, forcing the established players to play catch up at a game with which they are not familiar" (Norton & Pine, 2009, p. 5).

Leaders also may lose focus on the innovation that gave their organization a competitive advantage. Norton and Pine (2009) described this as experience innovation, where an organization constantly builds on gained experience to innovate. For instance, Walt Disney Company was an early pioneer of melding technology with family amusement. This disruptive innovation caused change in the movie and entertainment industry. Disney used its family focused experience innovation to build an empire. When Disney extended its reach beyond this narrow scope and attempted to add adult entertainment to its mix, the efforts failed, and Disney leaders had to reexamine the organization's long-term focus (Norton & Pine, 2009).

Tucker (2010) argued that complex systems showed early warning signs before disruptive change occurred. Research suggests these signs come in forms such as a noticeable slow-down in an area in the system or flickering, where the system may begin to show signs of changing (Tucker, 2010). The argument by Tucker (2010) confirms the need for leaders to become proactive and set up a culture in the organization that recognizes potentially disruptive change before the change occurs.

Employee readiness for disruptive change supports the need for proactive leadership. Aitken and Morgan (1999) stated that organizational leaders needed to create a resilient workforce that could handle the disruptive change seen in the environment. Resilience points to an individual's "ability to absorb high levels of disruptive change while displaying minimal dysfunctional behavior" (Aitken & Morgan, 1999, p. 54). This dysfunctional behavior may imply an employee becoming ill or his or her productivity dwindling. Leaders must create a culture that embraces change and promotes resiliency. Employees who can bounce back quickly and continue to work effectively will best promote the organization's long-term interests.

Futurology

Future studies date to the Sumerians. Throughout history many philosophers and scientists have researched the phenomena of why change occurs. For instance, the Pharaohs believed anticipating future events such as floods justified their power (Joseph, 2007). Other great thinkers such as Pythagoras, Socrates, Plato, Aristotle, and Bacon continued future studies through the ages (Joseph, 2007). Although supported by many well-known historical figures, future studies did not take hold until the mid-twentieth century when scientists began developing methods to anticipate military technology and nuclear disaster (Joseph, 2007; Toffler, 1972).

Anticipatory sciences, or futurology, have roots in efforts by the Rand Corporation's 1950s development of a model for the U.S. Air Force (Joseph, 2007). Rand Corporation scientists Olaf Helmer and Norman Dalkey co-created the Delphi method in the 1950s to identify change and understand what may cause future events (Joseph, 2007; Toffler, 1972). The Delphi method was a means to forecast long-range events that require the insight of more than one individual (Tersine & Riggs, 1976). Delphi addressed the problems associated with groups and potential research bias by using anonymous expert participants for completion of questionnaires rather than conducting in-person group sessions (Tersine & Riggs, 1976). Mullen (2003), citing Linstone and Turoff (1975), described the Delphi method as "structuring a group communication process so that the process is effective in allowing a group of individuals, as a whole, to deal with a complex problem" (p. 37). The Delphi method has expanded into many industries and fields beyond military applications including health care (Mullen, 2003).

Joseph (2007) stated an important construct in anticipatory thinking was basing forecasts on hard evidence, not opinion. According to Joseph (2007), the science of futurology and forecasting has six steps:

1. Describe the change;

2. Identify why change may occur;

3. Identify the influence of the change or results;

4. Identify the positive and negative benefits of change;

5. Identify the threats and opportunities of change; and

6. Develop strategy to manage change.

Many forecasts in the twenty-first century correlate with technology and note the influence technology can have on future decision-making and strategy development. The Internet revolution is a good example of how quickly technology can garner influence and become readily available and accepted by the mass populace. Some past technological advances, such as the radio, took decades to reach deep into American culture (Nichols, 1999). McLean (2007) argued technology was creating new paradigms for business and the development of strategy; walls were falling down and the boundary-less organization was becoming reality. All organizational leaders must become futurists and design infrastructures in their respective organizations to allow these coming challenges (McLean, 2007).

Mann (2010) stated that leaders should become futurists instead of planners to overcome the challenges created by the rapidly changing business environment. Leaders can no longer rely on the same strategies for long-term results. Environmental change causes leaders to change even the most carefully devised plans. History has been full of technological innovation that caused changes to occur in the environment, such as the steam engine, and the gasoline engine (Mann, 2010). The difference between yesteryear and today is the pace of change (Mann, 2010). Change historically has taken a generation to influence business (Mann, 2010). Technological innovation in the twentieth century destroyed this trend and provided a new paradigm supporting systems thinking and organizational change theories.

Garland (2007) posed a similar argument to Mann (2010) when he argued for leaders to use foresight and a systems approach. Leaders in the twenty-first century must consider not only the future of their organizations, but also the future of others (Garland, 2007). These considerations include monitoring trends in industries that may not directly correlate to their own industries (Garland, 2007). The idea of change extends typical models used by leaders, and creates new paradigms that leaders need to consider to ensure future success and competitive advantage. For instance, in the twenty-first century, leaders are facing new foes such as complete industry change, a stark comparison to the engrained idea of substitute products and new competitors (Garland, 2007). The speed of change is forcing leaders to deal with its influence because of its direct effect on their organizations. Leaders can no longer ignore trends or environmental change because doing so may affect their long-term survival (McLean, 2007).

Holistic Management

Knowledge management and using the full resources of the organization are becoming critical for survival in the twenty-first century. Vorakulpipat and Rezgui (2008) stated that organizations who took advantage of the collective knowledge found internally and through relationships with external sources might create a sustainable competitive advantage. This idea of collective knowledge reinforces the idea of systems thinking and promotes a holistic viewpoint of the firm.

Major employers worldwide are recognizing the value in promoting active employee participation in efforts toward creating a competitive advantage. For instance, Hewlett Packard (HP) and Wal-Mart each use employee participation to drive innovation and sustainability efforts (Aaron, 2010). Research suggests reduced employee turnover and higher employee productivity when leaders use holistic management strategies (Comeau-Kirschner & Wah, 1999).

Van Buren (2008) explored how the concepts of relational wealth or social capital applied to competitive advantage in an organization. This ideology also supports a holistic or systems approach to leadership. According to Van Buren (2008), relational wealth explained that leaders could create a competitive advantage by synergizing the organizations intangible assets: (a) employees, (b) suppliers and other external alliances, and (c) the organization's reputation in the marketplace. For organizations to exploit social capital, two values must exist in the organization: associability and trust. Van Buren (2008) defined associability as employees consciously deciding to make collective goals their primary focus. Trust comprises two concepts, fragility and resilience. Fragility relates to short-term benefits, explaining why some organizations have high employee turnover; employees leave the organization when the fragile trust no longer exists (Van Buren, 2008). Resilient trust has long-term implications as employees have multiple ties to the organization that garner their trust (Van Buren, 2008). Leaders must develop resilient trust to promote social capital (Van Buren, 2008).

Tuominen (2000) created a holistic management model that showed organizational interdependence as a merger of four important management models: (a) strategic, (b) product, (c) process, and (d) development. Tuominen (2000) argued that organizational success hinged on leaders recognizing the interdependence and influence all business functions had on each other; leadership needed to learn to manage the whole. How organizational leaders manage all processes may influence customer satisfaction and, more important, profitability (Hostetler, 2010).

Delen and Al-Hawamdeh (2009) identified four reasons leaders in the twenty-first century were promoting knowledge management and holistic ideas in their organizations:

- Technology was streamlining the learning process and making knowledge accessible;
- The amount of information available to leaders and their organizations was enormous;
- The workforce was shifting as the Baby Boomer generation began to retire; and

- A competitive advantage was necessary to give the
  organization an edge over its' marketplace opponents.

Plant (2008) offered similar advice when he stated that leaders must use

a holistic framework when creating a strategic plan to ensure

sustainable success. The plan should "be a living strategic plan that

encompasses all components of the planning process," otherwise "the

plan will simply gather dust and have no impact on the organizational

decision-making process" (Plant, 2008, p. 17). Leaders using systems

thinking need to draw together all organizational processes and create a

synergistic approach.

Theodore and Bronson (1987) analyzed a U.S. based company

in the apparel industry whose leadership made a conscious decision to

streamline operations to avoid moving production overseas. The

organization's leaders, according to Theodore and Bronson (1987),

used a holistic management approach, harnessing the abilities of every

department to streamline operations, reduce overhead, and increase

profitability and competitive advantage. The collective knowledge of

the organization helped the company increase productivity 19 percent,

and save millions in overhead costs (Theodore & Bronson, 1987).

Successful change programs require four fundamentals:

- Leaders who understand that success does not happen
  because of one person;

- Integration of company departments and efforts—a systems or holistic approach;

- Employee involvement in the decision-making process because employees are the driving force behind making change happen; and

- Organizational culture that promotes collective thinking (Theodore & Bronson, 1987).

Change does not magically happen, but rather change is the result of conscious efforts by leaders to transform the organization (Adcroft, Willis & Hurst, 2008). Adcroft, Willis, and Hurst (2008) created a model to show how change occurs in organizations using a systems viewpoint. The speed and complexity of change demands that leaders use all resources available. The model presented by Adcroft, Willis, and Hurst (2008) helps explain the synergistic advantages of holistic decision-making in the organization. According to Adcroft, Willis, and Hurst (2008) three areas contributed to the transformation process in organizations: (a) the event, (b) the strategy to make the transformation reality, and (c) the resulting transformation. Understanding each step in the change process allows leaders to refine strategy, and harness organizational learning. Perhaps more important, the model shows the linkage between organizational resources, and how leaders must understand how the resources fit together to create the change.

Leaders who want to promote a systems approach should consider how employees view spiritual, intellectual, and emotional influences. Stebbins (2010) examined an expanded version of holistic thinking called reality system theory. Stebbins (2010) suggested employee productivity correlates with three influences:

- Spiritual inspiration—employees view challenges as spiritually motivating;

- Intellectual innovation—the problems challenge employee intellectual ability; and

- Emotional conversation—describes how employees receive emotional stimulus through communication.

When these three realities exist for employees, the result is an organizational culture that fosters creativity and proactive thought (Stebbins, 2010).

Intentional Change Theory

Boyatzis and McKee (2006) argued that individuals who intentionally managed their personal development could achieve higher satisfaction and transformation capabilities. Leaders who understand that change begins with the individual may unlock sustainable leadership and change in their organization (Boyatzis & McKee, 2006).

This purposeful intent is the foundation for self-directed learning, known today as intentional change theory (ICT).

Research suggests five discoveries may lead to personal sustainable change (Boyatzis & McKee, 2006; Oosten, 2006):

- The ideal self—describes an individual recognizing who he or she wants to become;

- The real self—identifying who the individual is today;

- The learning agenda—identifying how to learn to become the ideal self;

- Experimentation and practice—carrying out the learning agenda; and

- Developing personal relationships—relationships that support and help change occur.

The Boyatzis (2006) theory of self-directed learning also provides a basis for an organizational approach to intentional change. Oosten (2006) expanded on the Boyatzis (2006) theoretical framework to include organizational change. Oosten (2006) used appreciative inquiry (AI) to show how organizations can create long-term sustainable change. AI requires identification of organizational strengths, and use of those strengths to create change (Oosten, 2006).

Oosten (2006) stated leaders could not maintain change without intending to do so. Leader intent determines his or her control over organizational change (Oosten, 2006). Understanding how to identify current organizational capability or the 'real-self' from the employee level may be integral to creating sustainable change in the organization (Taylor, 2006). Without the intent to learn and transform oneself into something different, employee sustainable change efforts may fail (Taylor, 2006). The same axiom may hold true for organizational sustainable change efforts.

Boyatzis and Akrivou (2006) stated that a person's vision determines the ideal self. According to Boyatzis and Akrivou (2006), the ideal self has three parts: (a) a future vision, (b) hope the vision may become reality, and (c) a firm understanding of one's ability to make the vision reality. Howard (2006) expanded on the Boyatzis framework by suggesting that a person's emotions may influence intentional change. Employee behavior relies on two triggers, positive emotional attractors (PEAs) and negative emotional attractors (NEAs) (Howard, 2006). PEAs support employee motivation to change, and NEAs detract from this motivation (Howard, 2006). PEAs and NEAs play an important role in the discovery process outlined by Boyatzis and McKee (2006) and Oosten (2006). Howard (2006) stated that PEAs were the vision and dreams of the discovery equation process. These visions and dreams create the foundation for individuals creating the ideal self and, more important, intentional change (Howard, 2006). NEAs conversely detract from employee intent and represent human tendencies to fear the unknown (Howard, 2006).

Leaders who promote intentional change must identify PEAs and promote these stimulants in the organization. Perhaps through PEA, identification and support leaders can minimize employee resistance, and create sustainable change. The PEA argument by Howard (2006) may confirm earlier work by Kurt Lewin; Lewin's force-field analysis described leaders working to reduce resistors to change.

Resource-based Theory

Porter (1985), in *Competitive Advantage: Creating and Sustaining Superior Performance* stated that competitive advantage is a derivation of many pieces and parts in an organization. To assess competitive advantage accurately, leaders must consider individual organizational activities and their interactions with each other (Porter, 1985). Drucker (1999) stated that how leaders used their scarce resources such as people and capital would determine if organizations failed or succeeded. Dissecting the organization according to strategic activity can help leaders identify areas for differentiation, and the relationship of these activities to relevant costs (Porter, 1985). Porter called this activity the value chain propositions.

Porter and his value chain propositions helped form the foundation for resource-based theory (RBT) (Olavarrieta & Ellinger, 1997). Porter posited strategies to create profits might include identifying the right industry, and creating a competitive advantage in the chosen industry (Olavarrieta & Ellinger, 1997). Effectively using the firm's resources to create this advantage is integral to the value chain strategy. According to the value chain propositions, a competitive advantage "is the firm's ability to create and appropriate more value than the competition" (Sheehan & Foss, 2009, p. 242). Porter argued that all activities need careful consideration, but should use a systems rather than departmental approach. These value chain activities include organizational strategy and effective use of change management.

Organizational agility also plays a role in the value chain propositions. Agility describes organizational ability to react to environmental change (Joroff, Porter, Feinberg & Kukla, 2003). The environmental challenges present in markets require leaders to construct agile organizations to overcome those challenges (Olavarrieta & Ellinger, 1997). Constant improvement of organizational processes can help create agility. For instance, the Toyota Production System (TPS) showed how process improvement could create agility in manufacturing operations (Joroff et al., 2003). Perhaps more important, agility supports with the value chain propositions, a systems approach to competitive advantage. For instance, no organization or process in the organization is an island, but rather each is dependent on many other processes occurring internal and external to the firm. How an organization reacts to these internal and external forces, or how agile the organization is, may determine future competitive advantage. Porter's ideology of driving value from individual organizational processes working together helps explain the systems approach to understanding the strategy behind resource-based theory.

Alsaaty and Harris (2009) viewed firm resources as a means to promote innovation, take advantage of opportunity in the marketplace, and create a sustainable competitive advantage. Furrer, Sudharshan, Thomas, and Alexandre (2008) added that long-term organizational success hinged on the ability of the firm to make and use its resources more uniquely than competitors. The challenge for leaders is to identify how to harness these resources and compel the resources into a synergistic alignment. Learning how to align resources for maximum benefit is becoming commonplace in corporate strategy (Joroff et al., 2003). Understanding what resources are, and the role resources play in the firm, may provide insight into this alignment challenge.

Olavarrieta and Ellinger (1997) stated organizations were groups of tangible and intangible resources, and identified three forms of resources:

- Input factors—raw resources the firm gains from the market, such as equipment or employee specific skills that when used in operations become an organizational asset;

- Assets—the tangible or intangible inventory or input factors under the organizational umbrella such as the brand names or patents a company owns; and

- Capabilities—the skill-based assets the organization controls. For instance, Wal-Mart has capability in distributing product within the Wal-Mart chain worldwide.

This description by Olavarrieta and Ellinger (1997) supported the Joroff et al. (2003) agility argument by confirming the natural progression of assets to become a flexible and agile organization. Successful organizations are constantly evolving and learning. Learning or using the resource equates into enhanced capabilities that become more difficult for competitors to copy (Olavarrieta & Ellinger, 1997). Low and Kalafut (2002) added that twenty-first century organizations faced with global competition were increasingly dependent on using intangible resources to create value. Innovation and agility are intangible resources competitors may find difficult to copy. The

obvious result may be a more agile organization and the creation of a
sustainable competitive advantage in the marketplace.

Competitive Advantage and Innovation

Many definitions exist in the literature for competitive
advantage. Porter (1985) believed firms created a competitive
advantage by delivering better value from processes in the organization
than did their competitors. Lucia (2008) stated a competitive advantage
was the firm's ability to create products and services superior to those
of competitors. Hamel and Prahalad (1994) saw competitive advantage
as a result of how leaders managed corporate challenges such as quality
or foreign market penetration. Low and Kalafut (2002) offered an
alternate approach by arguing that how leaders maximized value from
intangible resources might determine competitive advantage. Perhaps
the one common theme in each definition is the need for innovation.
Whether trying to extract value from scarce resources, designing new
products or services, or identifying new methods to solve business
challenges, leaders need to innovate better than their competitors.

Moore (2005) saw innovation as a necessity for survival and for
a sustainable competitive advantage. Lucia (2008) stated that
innovation was the single source of organizational survival in global
markets. Leaders face increased challenges every day because of global
competitiveness and rapid change; survival will depend on how quickly

the organization can adapt and innovate (Moore, 2005). If the organization can innovate faster than their competitors the firm may create a sustainable competitive advantage (Moore, 2005). Moore (2005) prefaced his argument by using Darwin's theory of evolution, linking the organic-based theory to business markets. According to Moore (2005), Darwin's theory applied to free market-based economies because:

- Scarce resources cause organizations to innovate to meet customer demands;
- Survival-of-the-fittest resulted from how consumers showed preference for certain innovations;
- Innovation would continue to grow more complex as organizations and markets evolved, raising the competence bar; and
- Leaders who failed to promote constant innovation and develop new skills would risk their organization becoming sub-par to its competitors.

Galan, Monje, and Zuniga-Vicente (2009) believed competitive advantage, taken from a small to medium enterprise (SME) perspective, could easily be applied to any size organization. SMEs often can innovate and adapt to change faster than their larger counterparts, but still fail more often (Galan et al., 2009). Mitigating this risk of failure means the organization must adopt a new, more flexible hierarchical structure that can respond to a quickly changing environment; the organization must learn to innovate and multitask (Galan et al., 2009).

> Organizations that operate in this way are usually thought of as ambidextrous…on one hand, hosting multiple, internally inconsistent architectures, competencies and cultures, with built-in capabilities for efficiency, consistency and reliability, and on the other hand using experimentation, improvisation and luck. (Galan et al., 2009, p. 66)

Hammer (2004) offered a different perspective on innovation by looking beyond products and services and focusing on how an organization operated. How leaders operate their organizations can influence all areas of the firm. Most leaders do not see operations as a means to creating a competitive advantage because operations are not visible in most organizations (Hammer, 2004). Leaders usually focus on higher level initiatives and neglect the organization's heart, operations (Hammer, 2004).

Many organizations have used operational innovation as the cornerstone for long-term success and competitive advantage. For instance, Wal-Mart's operations abilities in how the company distributed products proved a formidable challenge to competitors like Kmart and Sears to copy, helping Wal-Mart secure a leadership position in the highly competitive retail market (Hammer, 2004). Progressive Insurance, Toyota, and Dell are other good examples. Progressive leadership changed their claims processing procedures and in doing so reinvented the wheel, causing other competitors to be at a disadvantage (Hammer, 2004). Toyota's Production System and Dell's Business Model further exemplify how operations innovation can become difficult for competitors to copy and create a competitive advantage (Hammer, 2004).

Perhaps the greatest challenge for leaders is to identify how to leverage their organizations' resources to maximize value and create a competitive advantage. Harper and Glew (2008) expanded on this challenge by identifying three perspectives leaders must consider to promote a high achieving organizational culture:

- "Anticipatory perspective"—describes an organizations support for identifying change, including the ability to embrace change initiatives and learn;
- "Proactive mindset"—explains how some organizations lead their industry by promoting and creating change in their fields; and
- "Execution orientation"—leaders who can execute remain one-step ahead of their competition by knowing how to turn initiatives from vision to reality (p. 22).

Arora (2003) offered a similar perspective to Harper and Glew (2008) when he identified theory zyx.

According to Arora (2003), theory zyx has three axes, axis Z–planning, axis Y–execution, and axis X–people. Leaders must be able to plan for change, and in doing so create a vision and strategy to achieve the desired results. Likewise, without the ability to execute strategy, even the best plans and most innovative vision may never become reality. Finally, organizations need qualified people to lead the charge, and fight the battle on the ground; this takes leaders and soldiers. Effective military leaders make sure their troops receive good training, and so must leaders in business organizations; training is integral to readiness.

Arora (2003) called for deductive leaders in the organization. Deductive leaders envision the result and create a strategy to achieve this goal, essentially working backward from the finish to the beginning (Arora, 2003). This mentality helps overcome the limits of inductive thinking that permeates the corporate world and limits strategic thinking; most leaders are inductive thinkers (Arora, 2003). Deductive thinking allows leaders to think outside the box and promote innovative ideas that may seem beyond the norm. Inductive thinking limits innovation by causing leaders to see the present and not the future. Arora (2003) described managers as inductive thinkers, but effective leaders as deductive.

Each argument for a competitive advantage requires innovation, and points to leaders being aware of organizational capabilities and creating a synergistic environment that promotes and accepts change. Whether using an operations approach, one linked to a flexible structure, or simply creating products or services that offer more value than competitors, each strategy requires support from the entire organization. No department is an island, but rather an integral part of a larger complex system serving a higher purpose (Meadows, 2008). These pieces and parts working together as a system in the organization create the ability for the organization to meet strategic goals (Meadows, 2008). For instance, in a manufacturing company, marketing generates the sale, but without production to make the product and shipping to get the product from the plant to the customer, the marketing effort, no matter how skilled, is futile. The synergistic workings of an entire organization create a sustainable competitive advantage for the firm.

Current Findings

Leong and Jarmoszko (2010) argued leaders in the twenty-first century are facing challenges typical organizational structures and leadership styles used in the 20th century may not handle adequately.

Challenges such as information technology and a paradigm shift in the availability of knowledge across a global scale are forcing leaders to transform their organizations into highly adaptable entities (Leong & Jarmoszko, 2010). Organizational leaders must learn how to prepare their organizations for constant change. Perhaps the most important factors in this adaptability are how leaders manage their information and human capital (Leong & Jarmoszko, 2010).

President Dwight D. Eisenhower defined leadership as "the art of getting someone else to do something you want done because he wants to do it" (Billick, 2001). Employee buy-in is integral to the change management process. Reducing employee resistance to change may determine organizational adaptability success.

Wright (2010) offered insight into how leaders may reduce employee resistance through planning and good communication. According to Wright (2010), encouraging employee participation in the change process and effectively communicating a realistic vision to employees may help leaders overcome stifling resistance. Education is another tip offered by Wright (2010). For instance, leaders who manage change must become educated in change strategy to effectively lead those who will carry out the change; anyone working on the change must be knowledgeable of the process (Wright, 2010).

Galagan (2010) identified a gap in employee skills to meet twenty-first century job demands. This skills gap may hinder organizational ability to achieve long-term goals. Research by the American Society for Training and Development (ASTD) revealed a significant skills gap in organizational preparedness (Galagan, 2010). The ASTD reported that 79.2 percent of surveyed organizations reported a severe gap in skills needed to meet future challenges (Galagan, 2010). Leaders desiring a competitive advantage should work to fill this void (Galagan, 2010).

Becoming a change leader may be the new focus of the twenty-first century organization. Drucker (1999), in *Management Challenges for the 21st Century*, defined a change leader as an organizational, not individual leadership function. Everyone in the organization when working as a system creates, implements, and manages change. Recognizing that change creates opportunity is integral to achieving change leader status (Drucker, 1999).

Drucker (1999) stated that becoming "a change leader requires the willingness and ability to change what is already being done just as much as to do new and different things" (p. 74). To accomplish this Drucker (1999) suggested to:

- Stop allocating resources to non-producing processes;

- Continuously improve organizational processes in all departments;

- Take advantage of opportunities and expand on success; and

- Stress innovation and creating change throughout the organization.

These suggestions by Drucker (1999) may lay the foundation for competitive advantage by effectively using organizational resources.

Christensen (2010) supported the arguments by Porter (1985) and Drucker (1999) when he related organizational competitive advantage to value. Christensen (2010) stated competitive advantage is linked to value the organization provides customers. This extension of Porter's (1985) value chain propositions shows a systems approach to twenty-first century leadership.

Conclusion

The literature review showed leadership in the twenty-first century requires an innovative approach that recognizes internal and external systems' influences. Competitive advantage is a derivation of whatever the organization can do better than competitors such as create more value from processes (Lucia, 2008; Porter, 1985). Perhaps the greatest challenge for leaders is recognizing the change forces that influence the organization and adequately preparing the organization to manage these forces.

Hamel (2000) stated that survival depends on leaders straying from the status quo and thinking outside-the-box. Leaders who avoid following precedence, and instead seek to lead their organizations using a futuristic mentality may overcome the challenges associated with today's business environment (Hamel, 2000). Hamel (2000) argued the most effective leaders will focus on realistic change in their organizations, avoiding speculation. Leaders must imagine change before making the change reality (Hamel, 2000). "Companies fail to create the future not because they fail to predict it but because they fail to imagine it" (Hamel, 2000, p. 120). This revolutionary style leadership espoused by Hamel (2000) exemplifies the demands of the twenty-first century leader, the need to become a thought leader.

Summary

Chapter two provided a synergistic view of the literature. The literature review supported the idea that systems exist everywhere, and occur inside and outside the organization. Leaders who want to transform their organizations into learning entities and use change management to create a competitive advantage must recognize systems validity. The literature review provided the foundation for the current research by showing the link between change management and competitive advantage. Leaders who can create change in their organizations may create a sustainable competitive advantage.

Each theory encompassed in the literature review points to a common theme, the influence of internal and external forces on the organizational system. These forces may be systems themselves, existing inside and outside the organization. Success depends on leaders using the organization's tangible and intangible resources to their fullest ability to maximize value offered.

Chapter three will explain the research design for the study. The chapter will delve into the population and sampling, how the Delphi panel questionnaire design will gather data, offer a definition of consensus, and provide criteria for data analysis. The chapter will also finish laying the foundation and guide the data collection process for the current research study.

3 Method

The purpose of the current descriptive qualitative study was to explore change management methods and strategies used by seven leaders in the U.S. metal building industry. Integral to the study was the application of change management toward the creation of a competitive advantage. The questionnaire research design was based upon the Delphi method.

The Rand Corporation created the Delphi method in the 1950s for military forecasting (Grisham, 2009; Padel & Midmore, 2005). The method gathers data on a subjective and complex topic by polling a panel of experts, and a central mediator reviews the data for consensus (Grisham, 2009; Padel & Midmore, 2005). Grisham (2009) stated the Delphi method was scientific and could reveal insight into areas in which quantitative analysis may fail, and the technique provides a high degree of forecasting accuracy.

The Delphi panel of leaders from seven companies in the U.S. metal building industry met the following: (a) minimum of 10 years executive level industry experience, and (b) work for an organization operating for a minimum of 10 years. The study identified candidates from membership in the Metal Building Manufacturer Association (MBMA) and listings from the 2010 Metal Directory and Resource

Guide, published by Metal Construction News (MCN). The study attempted to identify two executives in each qualified organization who met the experience criteria, thus creating two lists. Leaders from up to 141 organizations in the U.S. metal building industry received invitations to take part in the study (see Appendix A for a list of potential organizations, and Appendix B for the individual request for participation).

The invitation process occurred in four rounds, beginning with the first list of qualified executives. The rounds continued until the candidate lists were exhausted. Once the selection process was complete, the data gathering process began. Data gathered supported a model that industry leaders could use to forecast, implement, and manage future change that may create competitive advantage.

Chapter three will describe the methodology and research design for the study. The chapter will review the instrument to gather data including population criteria for Delphi panel selection and how data collection will occur. A review of the data analysis process and identification of consensus will close the chapter.

Research Method and Design Appropriateness

The intent of the research study was to identify how leaders in the U.S. metal building industry identify and manage change, and how this may translate into a competitive advantage for their organizations and the U.S. metal building industry. The qualitative study questionnaire design used the Delphi method to gather subjective data that may be difficult to discover with quantitative techniques. Because of the uniqueness of data collected, the data is not statistically relevant, making quantitative analysis unsuitable for the study.

Dobrovolny and Fuentes (2008) identified many differences between quantitative and qualitative analysis and what constitutes proper use of each methodology. Researchers use quantitative analysis to prove or disprove an assumption or hypothesis, and qualitative analysis to evaluate an unknown concept (Dobrovolny & Fuentes, 2008). The questionnaire research design and Delphi technique followed this construct and allowed the researcher to gather unique data that were unknown to the community. For this research study, the community referred to the U.S. metal building industry, industry in general, and the academic community.

The Delphi method was the data collection method for the study. Rand Corporation scientists created the Delphi method to help mitigate the problems associated with group decision-making (Tersine & Riggs, 1976). For instance, group decision-making can produce limited results because of the friction created by group interaction. Tersine and Riggs (1976) stated "that group processes often leave participants exhausted, discouraged, and frustrated because of endless meanderings and a lack of resolution" (p. 51).

The Delphi technique provides a data gathering format that allows the researcher to harness subjective or opinion-based data from a diverse group of individuals (Tersine & Riggs, 1976). These individuals when asked specific but open-ended questions about change management may reveal solutions that could help U.S. metal building industry leaders and their respective organizations. The qualitative method creates the foundation and flexibility to offer the latter results (Dobrovolny & Fuentes, 2008). Grisham (2009) identified seven tests to determine when to use the Delphi method over other data gathering methodologies:

- The researcher is trying to solve a problem that requires subjective data from a group of individuals;
- The collective of individuals brought together to study the problem may be diverse;
- The group of individuals identified to participate may exceed the number that can meet in the same location;
- Group meetings may be impractical because of scheduling, location of participants, and costs;
- The effectiveness of in person meetings increases with extra group communication;

- Anonymity is critical because of potential conflicts among group members; and

- Individual thoughts and ideas can help create study validity and bolster study results.

Population and Sampling

The population for the current qualitative descriptive research study is senior executives in the U.S. metal building industry. Tersine and Riggs (1976) stated a sample size of 10 to 15 participants is adequate depending on group homogeneity, although no guidelines dictate panel or sample size. Homogeneity for this study is uniformity in panel participants (Anonymous, 1996). Because the study used executives from the U.S. metal building industry and each participant met rigid criteria of industry experience and organizational tenure, the panel met the homogeneous definition.

The Delphi panel consisted of seven executives, each from different organizations and meeting the following: (a) have a minimum 10 years of executive level industry experience, and (b) work for an organization in business for a minimum of 10 years. The researcher identified potential candidates through Metal Building Manufacturers Association (MBMA) membership and the 2010 Metal Directory and Resource Guide, an annual industry publication by Metal Construction News (MCN). The MBMA member roster is available to the public at http://www.mbma.com/display.cfm?p=41&pp=4. The MCN

Resource Guide was mailed to researcher as part of his free

subscription to the publication.

Because of industry size, lessened by industry consolidation,

the potential existed for not obtaining enough panel members to reach

data saturation. To mitigate this risk, invitations were sent to qualified

executives from all industry manufacturers based in the United States.

The MBMA shows 42 member organizations and the MCN directory

identifies 99 organizations. To broaden the opportunity to reach an

adequate panel size, the researcher attempted to identify two qualified

executives from each organization; creating two lists of qualified

executives for possible study inclusion.

Invitations were sent in four rounds. Executives not

responding to the invitation received a second invitation followed by e-

mail or telephone inquiries. The rounds continued until the list of

qualified candidates was exhausted. Candidates requesting not to

participate had their names removed from the candidate list.

Each invitation included an individual consent form for the

executive to review, sign, and return to participate on the Delphi panel

(see Appendix B for the individual request for participation). The

invitations for research participation outlined the risks, research design,

and study objectives. The invitations also stated the anonymity of study participants and respective company information. Overall, 81

qualified candidates were identified, and sent invitations. Seven

candidates or 8.64% agreed to participate in the study by signing and

returning the individual consent form.

Informed Consent and Confidentiality

Participation in the study was voluntary, and each participant

remained anonymous to the Delphi group. Executives in the U.S.

metal building industry received invitations based on experience and

organizational tenure qualifications. Only qualified candidates received

the invitation letters and consent agreements. Before the informed

consent was sent to qualified candidates, the University of Phoenix

Institutional Review Board (IRB) reviewed the document including

study procedures. The study could not begin until approval by the IRB

was granted in writing.

The letters and consent agreements asked the candidates to

take part in the study and confirm their consent by signing and

returning the documents. To encourage participation, the letter offered

a copy of the research results to all candidates who agreed to participate

on the Delphi panel. The invitation outlined study intent and how

participating in the study may help identify change strategies that could

benefit the candidates' organization and the U.S. metal building

industry. The invitations also outlined the confidentiality of all participant data and a study plan to ensure participant anonymity beyond the term of the study. The researcher coded all participant responses to prevent any lapse in participant confidentiality, and the study included no reference to participants' names or their respective organizations. Study data will remain in a safety deposit box for three years and be destroyed after this date. Any study candidates not returning the invitation and consent forms voided participation in the study.

Data Collection and Instrument Questions

Tersine and Riggs (1976) identified questionnaires or individual interviews as the primary methods for gathering data in a Delphi based study. The current research study used a questionnaire to gather data from the seven U.S. metal building industry executives. The 13-part round one questionnaire (see Appendix C) asked questions about change management techniques and the relationship of change management to competitive strategy. The round one questionnaire correlated with and was based on the central question and four related sub-questions. The 13 questions were designed to elicit specific information regarding the ideas presented in the study research questions.

The data gathering process occurred in three rounds. A typical Delphi study consists of three rounds to gather data and reach consensus, but the number of rounds is flexible (Powell, 2003).

Grisham (2009) identified five steps in a typical Delphi study:

1. Validate instrument: A pilot study using a representative population sample;

2. Round one: Initial questionnaire;

3. Round one feedback: Evaluate data and report to panel participants;

4. Round two: Second questionnaire based on round one feedback; and

5. Round two feedback: Evaluate data and report to panel participants.

The process continues until the researcher determines consensus or the data reveals consistent answers from panel participants.

The first round gathered unstructured data using open-ended questions. According to Powell (2003), first-round data help identify common themes, and open-ended questions help identify rich data. The second round expanded on previous responses and becomes structured in format. Tersine and Riggs (1976) stated the second round seeks to clarify responses from round one by allowing panel participants to review the data collected. The researcher, using a multiple choice format, provided panel participants the responses for each question from round one, and allowed each participant to modify his or her answers based on these results. This format allowed the researcher to narrow answers, gather more accurate data, and "encourage opinion convergence" (Tersine & Riggs, 1976, p. 55). The third round followed the format for round two. The data collection rounds concluded once consensus was obvious.

Questionnaire delivery was via the Internet. Participants received an e-mail link to QuestionPro, an online questionnaire management tool. The e-mail gave participants one week to respond. If any participant did not provide the data before the deadline, the participant received a second e-mail reiterating the questionnaire link and time frame for participation. The participant received an extra week to respond. If any participant did not respond to the second e-mail, the participant did not participate in the round.

Internal and External Validity

The decision to use a qualitative rather than a quantitative approach was based on the subjectivity and unknown nature of the data sought in the study. The qualitative method is a tool for gathering subjective data (Borrego, Douglas & Amelink, 2009), and is accepted in the research communities (Cassell, Symon, Buehring, and Johnson, 2006). Because of the subjectivity of qualitative research, establishing internal and external validity was paramount for study success. Internal validity refers to data authenticity (Creswell, 1994), or accuracy.

External validity refers to generalizability (Creswell, 1994), or the ability to apply the results to another sample (Salkind, 2003).

Ensuring study validity, internally and externally, required the identification of techniques to promote credibility, transferability, and dependability of data. For internal validity, Creswell (1994) suggested testing feedback by allowing study participants to evaluate data and getting participants involved in all phases of the study. For external validity, identifying "limitations in replicating the study" can provide insight into study generalizability because of qualitative study uniqueness (Creswell, 1994, p. 159). To create internal validity, a pilot study was used to validate the instrument, and the Delphi technique was used to gather data. Reviewing study limitations including researcher assumptions created external validity.

Salkind (2003) described validity as testing the instrument to ensure desired data is measured. According to Sharp (2010), an expert panel can validate an instrument. To establish instrument validity, a pilot study took place before the Delphi panel study began. The pilot study used an expert participant who had significant management experience working in the U.S. metal building industry. To remove potential bias, the pilot study participant did not participate in the Delphi panel study.

Shank (2006) stated that data strength establishes validity. For instance, data gathered (a) directly from participants, (b) from trusted participants, and (c) in a private setting may strengthen data (Shank, 2006). The current questionnaire research study gathered data using the Delphi method. "Delphi is a method to systematically solicit, collect, evaluate and tabulate independent opinion without group discussion" (Tersine & Riggs, 1976, p. 51). Using the Delphi method to gather data may help strengthen data collected and create study validity. The Delphi technique allowed for constant feedback and evaluation by permitting study participants to anonymously review answers from other participants during each round.

Study limitations influence the generalizability of data and the ability to replicate the study. Important study limitations included: (a) the availability of a sample population, (b) the methods available for identifying the population and sample, (c) time constraints, (d) the online delivery instrument QuestionPro, and (e) the current financial climate. According to Creswell (1994), because each study is unique, the ability to replicate the study is limited. Understanding the researchers' assumptions and biases may "enhance the study's chances of being replicated in another setting" (Creswell, 1994, p. 159). For this study, researcher assumptions and biases were primarily based on the researcher's 16-year work history in the U.S. metal building industry.

Other general assumptions included that industry leaders (a) had the desire to create a competitive advantage for their organizations, (b) see value in change management, and (c) have change management strategies in place.

Data Analysis

Data analysis is the crux of the study, second only to data collection. Interpretation of data and identifying themes to postulate consensus was a challenging task requiring a defined structure and process (see Appendix D for coding and thematic process). Each round allowed the researcher to analyze the data, postulate themes, and reformulate questions to help the panel reach consensus. The researcher used NVIVO9 software to analyze the data for theme identification. NVIVO9 was used for theme identification for round one only because rounds two and three used a structured format using multiple-choice questions. Manual analysis was used to analyze data from rounds two and three.

The first round used an unstructured format with open-ended questions to produce previously unknown ideas from the panel. These responses provided the basis for future structured rounds that seek to increase accuracy and, more important, draw consensus among the panel. The structured format allowed panel participants to rethink their initial responses based on knowledge of results from previous rounds.

Deciding on consensus is an important step in data analysis because consensus will define conclusions drawn from the data. Consensus of data is subjective, rests on data interpretation, and "there seems to be no firm rules for establishing when consensus is reached" (Powell, 2003, p. 379). Strategies to determine consensus vary and add to the subjectivity inherent with the Delphi design and qualitative method. According to Powell (2003) and Tersine and Riggs (1976), a few common strategies include:

- Accepting the median average as consensus;
- Using a weighted average where panel members receive an expertise or credibility factor; and
- Establishing a percentage agreement.

For this study, consensus was met when any question caused at least 50% of panel participants to reach the same conclusion. Once the questions met this requirement, the rounds ended, and final analysis took place.

Summary

This chapter reviewed the research method and design, the instrument, population criteria and selection, and how data analysis and consensus of data occurred. The current research study collected subjective data from a panel of experts in the U.S. metal building industry. The qualitative method and Delphi research design were suitable for gathering subjective and opinion-based data (Tersine &

Riggs, 1976). Chapter four will report the results and provide an in-

depth analysis of the data.

4 Presentation and Analysis of Data

The purpose of this descriptive qualitative study was to explore change management methods and strategies used by leaders in the U.S. metal building industry. Questionnaires were conducted with a Delphi panel of seven leaders in the U.S. metal building industry. The questionnaire data analysis revealed common themes about change forces, methods, and strategies used by industry leaders to manage change in their organizations.

The central question providing the foundation for the study was: How do leaders in the U.S. metal building industry identify, manage, and translate change management into a competitive advantage for their organizations? The research sub-questions described in chapter one helped maintain study focus and provided the foundation for the survey design, data gathering, and analysis process. The research sub-questions included:

1. How do leaders in the U.S. metal building industry perceive change management and identify, recognize, and differentiate between internal and external change forces?

2. How do leaders in the U.S. metal building industry respond to internal and external change, and how do these forces affect their change management strategies?

3. How do leaders in the U.S. metal building industry define competitive advantage, and how does change management influence creating a competitive advantage?

4. How do responses of leaders in the U.S. metal building industry reflect systems thinking, and what theories outlined in the conceptual or theoretical framework do their responses support?

Chapter four presents the data analysis and summary of findings for the Delphi panel questionnaires. A pilot study was conducted prior to beginning the data gathering process. The intent of the pilot study was to confirm the round one survey questions, and the online data gathering platform, QuestionPro. After completion of the pilot study, the data gathering process began with seven Delphi panel participants.

The study required three questionnaire rounds to establish consensus. Data was analyzed after each round for common themes and to determine consensus among participant responses. Chapter four includes a detailed explanation of the data gathering process and data analysis, including how consensus was determined. The chapter specifically includes (a) sample or population demographics, (b) pilot study findings, (c) data collection procedures and survey response rate,

(d) data coding analysis, (f) presentation of data findings, (g) survey results, and (h) summary.

Sample Demographics

The population for the research study was senior executives in the U.S. metal building industry. The sample population was identified by using two industry sources, the membership list of the Metal Building Manufacturer Association (MBMA) and listings from the 2010 Metal Directory and Resource Guide, published by Metal Construction News (MCN). The criteria for the sample population was (a) have a minimum 10 years of executive level industry experience, and (b) work for an organization in business for a minimum of 10 years.

The Delphi panel consisted of seven senior executives, each from different organizations. The specific titles of the executives included: president (three or 43%), vice president (three or 43%), and owner (one or 14%). Participant leadership experience ranged from more than 25 years (two or 29%) to less than 25 years (five or 71%). All study participants were male and came from organizations based in the United States and in business for a minimum of 10 years. Participant organizations showed industry leadership represented by Metal Building Manufacturer Association (MBMA) membership (five or 71%).

Using the demographic data, the researcher verified each participant was qualified for the research study. Each participant had significant U.S. metal building industry leadership experience and had worked for an established industry organization. The demographic data supported the study need for senior leaders responsible for recognizing and developing change management strategies for their respective organizations.

Pilot Study Findings

A pilot study was conducted in early February 2011. Teijlingen and Hundley (2002) described a pilot study as a means to test a potential instrument, a step that may enhance study success. The intent of doing the pilot study was to validate the round one questionnaire and the QuestionPro Internet-based survey instrument. The round one questionnaire contained open-ended questions that sought to identify change management strategies and techniques used by leaders in the U.S. metal building industry. The pilot study contained 18 questions (13 round one questions and five questions pertaining to feedback for the questionnaire instrument) and was administered to one volunteer participant who met the similar criteria as the panel participants. The five feedback questions included:

1. Was the QuestionPro survey easily accessible and usage instructions clear?

2. Were the questions easy to understand?

3. Did the questionnaire structure flow correctly?

4. Would you add, change, or delete any questions?

5. What survey areas could be improved?

The questionnaire was sent to the pilot study participant using QuestionPro, an online delivery instrument. To maximize the pool of research study candidates, pilot study candidates were identified from supporting industries, such as consulting or construction management, but had significant leadership experience working for a manufacturer in the U.S. metal building industry. Invitations were sent to two pilot study candidates who met the criteria; each agreed to participate in the pilot study, but only one candidate returned the study consent form.

The pilot study participant completed the online questionnaire on February 9, 2011. The participant confirmed the questions were easy to understand and accessible, including the QuestionPro delivery platform. The participant also confirmed the questionnaire structure flowed correctly. The participant could not identify any questions that should be added, changed, or deleted. The participant did identify an area for improvement: the QuestionPro online delivery tool. The participant noted the QuestionPro platform allowed the participant to return only to the previous question, thereby limiting the participant's ability to review previous responses. To mitigate this, research study participants received notification about this QuestionPro limitation.

The pilot study participant validated the instrument and confirmed the instrument's questions were easy to comprehend and would gather the desired data from study participants. The participant also confirmed the QuestionPro platform has limitations but is a reliable means of gathering online data. QuestionPro offers a secure means to collect data using a convenient online medium, providing easy access to users regardless of location.

Data Collection Procedures and Survey Response Rate

Shank (2002) described "qualitative research as a systematic empirical inquiry into meaning" (p. 6). The description offered by Shank (2002) helps define the intent for this study: To gather data from executives in the U.S. metal building industry about change management methods and strategies. This study explored the methods and strategies by using a questionnaire instrument delivered online via QuestionPro.

The Delphi study population consisted of executives in the U.S. metal building industry. Study candidates were identified using membership in the Metal Building Manufacturers Association (MBMA) and listings from the 2010 Metal Directory and Resource Guide, published by Metal Construction News (MCN). The sample population met the following criteria: (a) a minimum of 10 years executive level industry experience and (b) worked for an organization operating for a minimum of 10 years. Each candidate's qualifications were confirmed by visiting their respective organization's websites.

The participant qualification process began by identifying potential organizations. The MBMA membership roster identified 42 potential organizations, and MCN, 99 organizations, for a total of 141 candidate organizations (see Appendix A). Each company identified was researched to verify study criteria qualification. The organization research yielded 77 exclusions. The exclusions included:

- 23 metal building brokers (i.e., non-manufacturers);
- 21 prior or existing relationship with researcher;
- Two organizations located outside the United States;
- 10 non-pre-engineered companies; and
- 21 miscellaneous (i.e., out of business or unable to locate information).

After exclusions, 64 organizations remained. From this pool of organizations, 81 potential study candidates were identified. An attempt was made to identify two qualified candidates from each organization.

On January 17, 2011, the first round of invitations was randomly sent to 25 qualified candidates. The invitation letter, "Informed Consent," outlined the intent of the research study and included study guidelines, potential risks, and benefits (see Appendix B). Candidates were assured anonymity and instructed to sign and return the document to the researcher. By signing the document, participants agreed to the terms and conditions outlined. The first round of invitations yielded one participant.

Round two invitations were sent on January 24, 2011 to 10 qualified candidates. On January 31, 2011, follow-up emails were sent to candidates from round one. The follow-up email resulted in four responses: two candidates did not have time for the study, one agreed to study participation, and one expressed interest.

Round three invitations were sent on February 7, 2011, to 15 candidates. Follow-up emails were sent the same day to round two candidates. Round four invitations were sent on February 8, 2011, and February 10, 2011, to 31 candidates; five were emailed, and 26 were sent via fax. Follow-up emails were sent on February 11, 2011, to round three candidates. Rounds three and four resulted in five candidates agreeing to participate in the study. Overall, 81 invitations were sent, and seven candidates agreed to participate in the study, resulting in a response rate of 8.64%. Each participant signed and returned the informed consent form and was assigned a unique participant code identifying their responses throughout the study and ensuring participant confidentiality.

On February 21, 2011, the research study officially began, and the round one questionnaire was sent to the seven individuals who agreed to participate. The round one survey contained 13 open-ended questions (see Appendix C). By February 26, 2011, three participants successfully responded to the survey. A follow-up email was sent to the remaining four participants on February 27, 2011. Six participants completed the round one questionnaire by February 28, 2011. The seventh individual who had initially agreed to participate did not respond, and was therefore excluded from the study, reducing the pool of participants to six. The response rate for the round one survey was 85.71%. Because of the high response rate, the decision was made to proceed with round one analysis and continue the study.

Data analysis for round one took place during the first week in March 2011. The round one questionnaire followed an unstructured format, using open-ended questions to gather data. Participant responses were coded according to their participant identification, such as participant 1, participant 2, and entered into NVIVO9 for analysis. Coding data assured participant anonymity. The participant responses were analyzed for common words or themes (a) using NVIVO9 word query (see Appendix E), and (b) manually by the researcher. The themes identified were used to create a structured multiple-choice format for the round two questionnaire. Using a structured multiple-choice format allowed the participants to review round one answers from all participants and reconsider their previous responses. The format also encouraged consensus among participants by narrowing the field of potential answers. Two additional questions were added to the round two questionnaire. The two open-ended questions asked participants to identify, in their opinion, the three greatest change forces that will face the U.S. metal building industry in the next (a) five to ten years and (b) 25 years, respectively. Round two contained 15 questions: 13 multiple-choice, and two open-ended questions.

Round two began on March 6, 2011, and was sent to six participants. To ensure study credibility, the seventh participant was excluded from the study because of nonparticipation during round one. By March 7, 2011, four participants had responded to round two. On March 10, 2011, a follow-up email was sent to the remaining two participants, resulting in an additional participant completing the questionnaire. Because of the high response rate, five out of six participants, or 83.33%, data analysis began after the fifth participant's response. By March 13, 2011, all participants had completed the questionnaire, and the sixth participant's responses were incorporated into the data analysis. The response rate for round two was 100%. The round two data analysis revealed consensus on nine questions, leaving six questions for round three. Round three followed a structured format and contained six multiple-choice questions.

The objective of round three was to identify consensus for the remaining six questions. Round three contained six questions and was intended to be the final data gathering round for the study. Participants were given the response rate expressed as a percentage for four questions, numbers one, two, three, and four. Providing response rates for each answer was meant to encourage consensus among participants. According to Tersine and Riggs (1976), when conducting a Delphi study, "the purpose of information feedback is to produce more precise predictions and to encourage opinion convergence" (p. 55). The remaining two questions, numbers five and six, pertaining to change forces, had such a wide array of answers from round two that it was not feasible to give percentages. Round three began on March 13, 2011, and the questionnaire was sent to six participants. By March 16, 2011, three participants had completed the questionnaire. On March 20, 2011, a follow-up email was sent to the remaining three participants. By March 27, 2011, four out of six participants, or 66.67%, completed the questionnaire. Because of the high response rate, the decision was made to end round three on March 28, 2011, and begin data analysis.

Data Coding and Analysis

Data analysis for the research study occurred after each round. The data analysis for round one involved three steps: (a) coding responses to the 13 questions, (b) inputting the data into NVIVO9 software to analyze the data for common themes, and (c) manually analyzing data. During coding, each response was coded to match the participant who created the response. For instance, the responses from participant one were coded participant 1. The NVIVO9 word query feature was used for thematic analysis. This step was necessary because round one followed an unstructured format using open-ended questions that revealed a wide range of answers. After themes were identified, manually reviewing each response and correlating the responses to each other and the common themes further analyzed participant responses. A new structured questionnaire following a multiple-choice format was created for round two using the data gleaned from the round one analysis. The questions were identical to round one, but the participants were given a fixed group of answers from which to select. The reason for doing this was to encourage participant consensus for each question. Two additional open-ended questions were added to the questionnaire, bringing the total survey questions for round two to 15. Round one did not reveal consensus for any questions.

Round two analyses followed a similar format, except the data were manually analyzed only. Because the survey primarily used a multiple-choice format, NVIVO9 was not needed for the analysis. The two open-ended questions, although producing a wide range of responses were analyzed easily because of the one-word answers given. Percentages were calculated for the answers given to each question to determine consensus. For the purpose of this study, consensus was determined to exist for any question in which at least 50% of participants show agreement. The analysis revealed that nine out of 15 questions met consensus among participant responses. The remaining six questions made up round three.

Round three was the final round of the research study data gathering process. The round contained six questions. The question wording did not change from the first or second rounds. To encourage consensus, participants were given the percentage response rate for each group of answers for questions one, two, three, and four. Data analysis for round three revealed consensus for the remaining six questions.

Presentation of Data Findings

Round One

The round one questionnaire (see Appendix C) used an unstructured format containing 13 open-ended text questions meant to gather unknown data from the Delphi panel participants; six out of seven participants, or 86%, completed the questionnaire. The participant responses were analyzed for common themes, and these data were used to construct the round two questions. Common themes evident in the round one data included:

(a) The need to constantly adapt to market conditions;

(b) The presence of economic conditions that force tough decisions such as downsizing;

(c) The need for good information from reliable sources;

(d) The need to develop responses to manage internal and external change; and

(e) Transforming change strategy into competitive advantage. The themes identified were consistent through the remainder of the study, and provided support for the *first-to-change mover triangle* (see *Figure 1*) presented in chapter five. Consensus was not determined for any question in round one, but did reveal significant insight for each question by the panel. For round one questions and responses, please see Appendix F.

The first question asked participants to define change management. Participant responses provided a basis used to develop a definition in round two and included:

- Participant 1: "The process of leading or guiding staff through modifying processes or procedures;"

- Participant 2: "Management that responds to the outside elements making changes reflective of the outside elements;"

- Participant 3: "Change management is a process that an organization or team within an organization uses to affect change or transition within the group from a current state to a desired state;"

- Participant 4: "Change management is the process of planning and executing actions that alter the direction of our company;"

- Participant 5: "Recognition of the need to adapt to altered conditions in the business environment and doing so in a thought out planned for way;" and

- Participant 6: "The ability to adapt one's style or organization to the constant changes being created by market demands, competition, product innovation, new communication systems, scarcity of resources or

government interference."

Question two asked participants to identify significant change

experienced in their organizations. Participants identified important

changes such as:

- Participant 1: "Scale down of business levels, thus reducing

  staff and increasing individual responsibilities over

  multiple areas of the business;"

- Participant 4: "Our revenues decreased 30% from 2008 to

  2009. We reduced headcount and actually sold a division

  to manage our cash and survive the Great Recession;" and

- Participant 5: "The need to survive in a period of

  diminished sales revenue and declining margins due to a

  drastic reduction in market activity."

Question three sought to identify what precipitated the changes

identified in question two. Participant responses such as "madness that

is currently the reality of the competitive bid market" (Participant 3),

"the banks stopped lending money" (Participant 4), and "turbulence in

financial markets" (Participant 5) signaled a clear link to the economic

environment creating the stimulus. Question four asked participants to

identify their methods for recognizing and forecasting change forces.

Participants offered a wide range of responses including: "word of mouth" (Participant 2) "bid history and win history" (Participant 3),

"concerns from our customers", "financial reports, and anecdotal

information from visitors to many businesses, such as vendors and

truck drivers" (Participant 5).

Question five asked the panel to explain how they differentiate

between internal and external change forces. Responses varied but

showed a clear understanding among the panel that external change

occurs outside the organization and internal within the organization,

and that external change forces may influence or create internal change.

Question six focused on what participants perceive caused internal

change in their organization. Notable responses included: "change in

ownership" (Participant 1), "external change forces" (Participant 2),

and "the result of pursuing success" (Participant 6). Question seven

asked participants how they responded to the internal change.

Responses included "adapted to the changes by trying to understand

the strengths of the changes and buying into the improvements"

(Participant 1), "the process involved many meetings" (Participant 3),

and "increased the amount of communication and focused more on

consensus management" (Participant 5). The responses may suggest

the participants view change management as a company-wide initiative

supporting a systems approach. Question eight examined external

change and what participants believe caused external change in their organizations. The economy appeared at the epicenter of responses. Question nine expanded on question eight by asking participants to identify how they responded to external change. Responses such as I became more aware of our financial plight (Participant 2), and "accepted additional responsibilities and roles" (Participant 1) showed a clear link to accepting leadership responsibility and becoming more involved in daily operations.

Question 10 attempted to gauge how participants perceive internal and external change influences managing change in their organizations. Responses indicated a significant influence, and the leaders perceived staying proactive in change management may help their organizations. Question 11 expanded on question 10 by asking participants how the change forces hinder or support their organizations ability to compete. Participant responses suggested that each believed that change forces influence their ability to be competitive in the marketplace. For instance, Participant 5 commented that "our changes are done only to support our ability to compete;" pointing to a belief that change is integral to competitive advantage. Question 12 asked participants to define competitive advantage. A sampling of responses used to form a new definition used in round two include:

- Participant 2: "A cost advantage over a competitor;"

- Participant 3: Flexibility;

- Participant 4: "What we do better than anyone we
  compete with;" and

- Participant 5: "A compelling reason to customers to
  purchase our goods."

Participant 6 included a five-step process when defining competitive advantage:

1. "define targeted needs,"

2. "meet those needs consistently,"

3. "stand up to customer evaluation,"

4. "achieve word-of-mouth endorsement," and

5. "create broad-based awareness".

Question 13 was the final question in round one. The question asked participants how they believed change management might create a competitive advantage for their organizations. Responses supported earlier assertions such as increased communication and team philosophy (Participant 1), reduced knee jerk reactions (Participant 5), and enhancing existing organizational competitive advantage(s) (Participant 4).

Round Two

Round two contained 15 questions, and six out of six participants, or 100%, completed the questionnaire (see Appendix G). Questions 2-11 and question 13 were identical to those in round one. Questions 1 and 12 were revised to offer participants a definition of change management and competitive advantage, respectively; two new questions were added to offer a future perspective to change issues facing the U.S metal building industry. The original 13 questions followed a structured multiple-choice format. The structured format was meant to encourage consensus among participants. The selection of multiple-choice answers for questions one to 13 was based on participant response analysis from round one. Questions 1 to 13 offered participants an opportunity to recommend further changes or additions to the selection of answers. The two added questions were open ended and asked participants to identify, in their opinion, the three greatest change forces facing the U.S. metal building industry both in the next five to ten years and in the next 25 years.

Analysis of round two data revealed that nine questions met consensus. For the purpose of this study, consensus is defined as any question in which at least 50% of participants show agreement. Because of the rich data gleaned from participants, it was felt that study rigor could be increased if the definition of consensus was modified to

require three responses for each question meeting at least 50%
agreement. This new definition was used on all questions except
questions 1 and 12, which asked participants to offer a definition of
change management and *competitive advantage*. For these questions,
consensus was determined when at least 50% of participant responses
were similar. For participants' responses to round two, please see
Appendix G.

The questions meeting consensus in round two included,
questions 1, 2, 3, 5, 6, 7, 9, 12, and 13. More than 50% of participants
agreed on the selected answers for these questions. Question one met
consensus because 83% of participants agreed on the following
definition of change management:

> Change management is a dynamically structured team process
> of planning and execution in which leaders recognize change
> and adapt the organization to meet altered conditions in the
> business environment, created by forces such as competition,
> product innovation, and scarcity of resources.

For question two, 100% of participants identified significantly reduced
revenue and margins, 83% cited downsizing such as headcount and
expenses, and 83% identified increased workloads on fewer employees
as significant change experienced in their organizations. Question three
revealed that 100% of participants viewed the economic environment,

66% mentioned the increasingly competitive bid market, and 66% acknowledged bank lending practices and financial market instability as precipitators of the changes identified in question two. Question five asked participants to identify how they differentiated between internal and external change forces. The consensus responses revealed that 66% of participants agreed that:

- External change influences the industry, and internal change affected only the organization;

- External change created the need for internal change;

- External change produced events beyond the control of the organization; internal change created events the organization might control; and

- Internal change was a result of the need for the organization to compete for customers, employees, and investors; external change results from the natural evolution of competitors, technology, and changing market conditions including government intervention.

In question six, 83% of participants identified reduced sales volume, heightened competitive environment, and response to external economic conditions to reduce expenses and increase efficiency as causes of internal change in their respective organizations. Question seven asked participants how they responded to internal change.

Consensus responses revealed that 83% evaluated changes and made necessary organizational adjustments, 66% increased communication in the organization, and 66% accepted change and looked for ways to maximize organizational benefit. Question nine sought to identify how the participants responded to external change. Participant responses identified that:

- 66% increased workload and responsibilities across all departments;

- 66% increased personal involvement in daily operations including financial management;

- 83% identified ways to reduce operating expenses including inventory levels and pricing; and

- 66% identified new product and service areas to increase potential customer base and organizational advantage.

Question 12 followed a similar format as question one and asked participants to define competitive advantage; 66% of participants agreed on the following definition:

A competitive advantage means flexibility, customer loyalty, and performing better than competitors. The organization will achieve a competitive advantage by reacting and adapting faster, listening to customer needs better and developing strategies to differentiate and compel customers to buy, recommend, and place a premium value on its products and services.

Question 13 was the final question meeting consensus in round two. The question asked participants how they believed change management might create a competitive advantage for their organizations. Responses revealed that 66% of participants agreed that change management:

- Increased communication in the organization;

- Promoted team philosophy;

- Would enhance existing organizational competitive advantage(s) by demanding constant improvement; and

- Supported the call for dynamic organizations that constantly adapted to customer and stakeholder needs, and rewarded employees for creating value in the organization.

Questions 4, 8, 10, and 11 also met consensus, but it was decided to include these questions in round three because the questions contained one or more answers showing only 50% agreement among participants. By including the questions in round three and eliminating any potential answers garnering more than a 50% response rate in round two, it was hoped round three would reveal a higher response rate among the remaining answer choices. The remaining six questions, numbers 4, 8, 10, 11, 14, and 15, formed the basis for round three. For round three, questions four and eight requested participants to select one answer because two answers previously achieved more than 50% consensus in round two, question 10 requested two answers, and questions 11, 14 and 15, three.

Some of the questions from round two also contained recommended changes or additions. For any question containing recommended changes or additions, the recommendations were analyzed for inclusion. If the recommended changes or additions were determined to not be similar to the existing answer selection, the changes or additions were made. Round three questions one and two contained changes because of participant-recommended changes or additions in round two. For question one, "steel prices versus substitution material prices," and "monitor government policies and regulations" were added to the answer pool. For question two, one answer was added, "raw material prices."

Round Three

Round three consisted of six questions (see Appendix H). Three of six participants completed the entire questionnaire; one completed questions one through five, skipping question six. The questions matched round two, but participants were given the response rate from round two for each possible answer. The response rate, shown as a percentage, was given for all questions except questions 5 and 6. These two questions contained a range of responses, and the percentages were considered insignificant. After incorporating the responses from round two that achieved more than 50% consensus, two answers for question four and eight, and one answer for question 10, consensus was determined for all round three questions.

Question one asked participants how they recognized or forecasted change forces. Participants identified word of mouth (100%), economic indicators such as housing and industrial statistics (50%), and customer buying behaviors and concerns (83%) as tools to recognize and forecast change. In question two, participants identified the economic environment (83%), a heightened competitive environment (50%), and changing customer buying patterns and behaviors (66%) as causes of external change in their organizations. Question three asked participants how they perceived internal and external change forces influenced managing change effectively in their organizations. For consensus,

- 50% of participants saw the change forces as a major influence because not managing the influences left organization open to failure;
- 66% agreed that managing the changes made them stronger and more competitive in a down market; and

- 75% agreed the change forces helped the organization become more focused on customer needs.

Question four expanded on question three and asked participants to identify how these change forces hindered or supported their organization's ability to compete. Responses included:

- 75% of participants agreed the change forces created a competitive advantage because their organization were constantly adapting to customer needs rather than reacting to change like many of their less prepared competitors;

- 100% agreed that company size allowed their organizations to take advantage of rapidly changing markets faster than competitors; and

- 75% believed the change forces created a heightened awareness of organizational capabilities and value-added services for their customers.

The final questions for round three focused on identifying future change forces. Question five asked participants to identify the three greatest change forces facing the U.S. metal building industry in the next five to 10 years. Participants agreed that availability of capital (50%), energy codes (75%), and government policies, including market manipulation, and tax laws (75%), represented the greatest change forces facing the industry short-term. In question six participants broadened the scope to include the next 25 years. Although participants identified 14 specific long-term change forces in round two, only one achieved consensus, government policies, with 66% in agreement; seven other selections received one vote each. These seven responses included: availability of skilled labor because of retiring labor force, energy codes, foreign competition, increase in alternative construction methods and products, new technology, raw material costs versus alternatives, and unstable domestic economy.

Questionnaire Results

The research study succeeded in identifying change management strategies and methods used by leaders in the U.S. metal building industry. The Delphi panel produced consensus after three rounds. This success confirmed the Delphi technique as an appropriate means of identifying and gathering unknown data. For a recap of study results please see Appendix I.

The first round identified a knowledge base used to create rounds two and three. Participant responses in round one identified a variety of data, and NVIVO9 word query helped pinpoint commonality and themes among responses (see Appendix E). The analysis also showed the responses were remarkably similar. This characteristic caused round two to garner a high percentage of consensus questions. For instance, in round two, 13 of 15 questions, or 87%, met consensus criteria. The decision was made to include four of the 13 round two questions meeting consensus in round three because questions, 4, 8, 10, and 11 contained participant responses showing only 50% consensus. Although these responses met the study definition of consensus, it was felt by including the questions in round three a higher percentage of consensus or data saturation could be met.

Round two offered an opportunity to narrow the survey responses and, at the same time, increase the richness of data gathered. The decision was made to add two questions to round two, bringing the question total to 15 for the round. This decision was made because round one data analysis showed an impressive array of responses, and because of this, the researcher believed the panel could offer further insight into the subject matter. The added questions also gave participants an opportunity to express their opinion of future change forces potentially impacting the U.S. metal building industry. This perspective caused a more rounded study outcome by creating a current and futuristic perspective for the U.S. metal building industry leadership.

Round three synergized previous round results and became the final round for the research study. The round provided consensus for the remaining six questions. The only question that did not garner more than one answer that met consensus was question six. The question asked participants to identify, in their opinion, the three greatest change forces facing the U.S. metal building industry in the next 25 years. During round two, participants identified 14 specific change forces ranging from availability of capital and new technology to government policies. Participant responses for this question were similar to the richness and content offered by participants throughout each round and in all questions, further confirming study validity.

The rounds produced consensus quickly. This achievement proved that although change management strategies and methods are complex subjects, leaders in the U.S. metal building industry have similar views on them. The questionnaire data analysis will continue in chapter five. The chapter will offer more in-depth analysis of questionnaire data, including recommendations for future research.

Summary

Chapter four presented the data collection process including how participants were qualified for the research study. This research study followed the Delphi technique, in which a group of expert participants, known as a panel, is questioned about a specific topic; the answers to the questions are unknown. The participant panel for this study represented an experienced group of leaders, ranging from senior executives to owners, in the U.S. metal building industry. The study success and the ease of reaching panel consensus confirmed the validity of the Delphi technique for gathering unknown data. Chapter five will

examine the data collected and draw conclusions for future study.

5 Conclusions and Recommendations

The purpose of chapter five is to identify conclusions and recommendations drawn from the data results in chapter four. The chapter will also include more in depth analysis of study results. The chapter contains nine areas, beginning with an overview of the research, and overview and interpretation of findings, in which the research method and design are reviewed and coupled with the research intent to show the importance of the study. Next, the chapter includes the study limitations, implications on leadership, and conclusions. The chapter ends with a discussion on recommendations for future study, recommendation for higher education, chapter summary, and researcher personal reflection.

Overview of Research

Organizations operating in the global environment of the 21st century are facing unprecedented challenges. Rapid technological advances are increasing the availability of information, raising the bar for leaders who must react faster and make changes quicker. Leader response time and how quickly the leader identifies the change forces, and implements strategy may determine future organizational competitive advantage. Leaders who innovate and take advantage of change may help their organizations survive (Cope, 2009). The challenges in the 21st century may be summed as how organizational leaders may become change leaders in their organization, industry, and communities.

French philosopher Diderot recognized in the 18th century the influence of change and availability of information on society when he stated:

> As centuries pass by, the mass of works grows endlessly, and one can foresee a time when it will be almost as difficult to educate oneself in a library, as in the universe, and almost as fast to seek a truth subsisting in nature, as lost among an immense number of books; then one would have to undertake, out of necessity, a labor that had been neglected, because the need for it had not been felt. (Diderot, 1755)

Diderot (1755) forecasted the challenges facing future society as technological changes improve access to information. These changes are creating a variety of "information overload," in which leaders struggle to balance the vast amount of information available when creating policy (Rosenberg, 2003, p. 1). Drucker (1999) stated that "change is unavoidable," and leaders "cannot manage change…only be ahead of it" (p. 73). Drucker (1999) used the latter context to define a change leader and the role a change leader plays in an organization. According to Drucker (1999), change leaders welcome change because they believe change creates opportunity and seek out change in the internal and external environment. Becoming a change leader means the leader will:

- Create policies in the organization to support future change;

- Design strategies to identify change in the environment;

- Create strategies to implement change at the organizational and external level; and

- Identify "policies to balance change and continuity" (p. 73).

The result of the Drucker suggestions is the opportunity to lead change. Landale (2004) confirmed the Drucker posits by stating that managers uphold norms in the organization, and leaders create change. The Drucker suggestions align with this research study's focus.

McAneny (2010) argued that leaders cannot implement change successfully if the organization is not prepared to accept the change. Using a United States Air Force perspective, described as a "Red is Good mentality," McAneny (2010) supported earlier assertions that change creates opportunity (p. 121). By using this "Red is Good mentality" and identifying areas needing to change, leaders create opportunities for the organization to become better; change is welcomed and not perceived as a threat (McAneny, 2010, p. 121). The

McAneny (2010) argument further cements the call for leaders to identify ways to create organizations receptive to constant change.

Perhaps the most succinct call for readiness to change came from a statement attributed to Darwin by Cope (2009): "It is not the strongest of the species that survives, nor the most intelligent that survives. It is the one that is the most adaptable to change" (p. 26). Darwin's point, although meant in a social context, helps explain the importance of adjustment or change in all facets of human life and easily applies to the organization. Darwin's statement also supports the need for this research study by adding claim to the need for all leaders to adopt and develop organizational adaptation.

Overview and Interpretation of Findings

The purpose of this research study was to identify change management strategies and techniques used by leaders in the U.S. metal building industry. Although the study research questions formed the basis for the study, the earlier Drucker (1999) suggestions provided support for the study survey question design and structure. The instrument questions were broken into four specific areas: change management, internal and external forces, competitive advantage, and future challenges. The first area, change management, sought to identify how U.S. metal building industry leaders define change management, their change experience, and how they have identified changes that effect their organization. The second area focused on internal and external change forces, how the leaders differentiated and responded to these forces, and the influence of the change forces on their ability to manage change and compete in the marketplace. The third area was about competitive advantage, how the leaders defined competitive advantage, and their perceived understanding of the relationship between change management and competitive advantage. The fourth area sought to provide a future outlook for the U.S. metal building industry by asking leaders to identify potential change forces facing the industry in both the next five to 10 years and the next 25 years.

Research study participants formed a Delphi panel of seven senior leaders in the U.S. metal building industry. The panel members each had (a) a minimum of 10 years executive level industry experience and (b) worked for an organization operating for a minimum of 10 years. A pilot study was conducted before the research study began to confirm the round one questionnaire and the Internet-based instrument delivery platform, QuestionPro. The pilot study consisted of one qualified individual with leadership experience in the U.S. metal building industry. The pilot study participant validated the round one questionnaire and the QuestionPro platform.

The first round of the research study was aimed at gathering unknown answers to 13 questions specifically related to change management. The questions, although generic, were meant to draw out the experience of the Delphi panel, a group of seven senior leaders in the U.S. metal building industry. The questions (see Appendix C) ranged from asking the Delphi participants to offer a definition of change management and competitive advantage to probing their experience when dealing with change management in their organization. Overall, six, or 85.71%, of the Delphi panel completed the round one questionnaire; one participant did not respond to the survey invitation. This participant was excluded from rounds two and three to reduce potential research bias in study data. The round one data was analyzed using NVIVO9 software, and the word query feature. NVIVO9 word query was used to identify the top 25 words used in participant responses (see Appendix E). Further analysis was completed by manually correlating the data with common words identified. Round one analysis did not reveal consensus for any questions but contained rich data used to create rounds two and three (See Appendix F).

Round two reiterated the 13 original questions to participants but in a multiple-choice rather than an open-text format (See Appendix G). The multiple-choice format was meant to encourage participant consensus. The multiple-choice selection for each question resulted from analysis of participant responses in round one. Round two also contained two new questions, which sought to identify participant perceptions of the greatest change forces facing the U.S. metal building industry in the next five to 10 years, and the next 25 years. The new questions were presented in an open-text format because the answers to the questions were unknown. Round two resulted in six participants or 100% of the panel completing the questionnaire. The data analysis identified nine questions or 60% that met consensus. The remaining six questions formed the basis for round three.

Round three contained six questions in a format similar to round two's (see Appendix H). Round three contained two differences from round two. The first was in the questions related to identifying future change forces; these questions were reformatted into multiple-choice questions. Another difference, offered solely to encourage consensus, was participants were provided the response rate, expressed as a percentage, for each multiple-choice answer from round two. Three panel participants completed round three in entirety, one completed all questions except number six, and two participants did not respond. Round three data analysis identified consensus for all questions, and was consequently the final round of the research study. For study consensus results, please see Appendix I.

The Delphi panel produced good results in round one by identifying a rich group of data. The round one data revealed that leaders in U.S. metal building industry have a working knowledge of change management strategies and methods. These data showed remarkable cohesiveness or similarity among panel participants even though consensus was not achieved. The most significant data came from questions one and 12, in which participants were asked to offer a definition of change management and competitive advantage, respectively. The round one data were strong enough to allow for the creation of a definition given to participants in round two:

- *Change management*—Change management is a dynamically structured team process of planning and execution, in which leaders recognize change and adapt the organization to meet altered conditions in the business environment created by such forces as competition, technology, and scarcity of resources.

- *Competitive advantage*—A competitive advantage means flexibility, customer loyalty, and performing better than competitors. The organization will achieve a competitive advantage by reacting and adapting faster, listening to customer needs better, and developing strategies to differentiate itself and compel customers to buy,

recommend, and place a premium value on its products
and services.

The definitions point to the belief among the panel participants that
change is an integral part of organization well-being, and the creation of
competitive advantage. Specifically, in the definition of competitive
advantage, change words such as *flexibility, adapting,* and *differentiate*
correspond with the notion of change management. Each definition
supports the arguments made throughout this paper about the need for
organizations that can quickly adapt and transform themselves to
maintain a competitive edge in the new global economy. Clearly, panel
participants recognized this need, as evidenced in the definition
formulated. Panel participants reached consensus on the definitions in
round two, with 83% and 66% of participants agreeing, respectively.

Round two data identified nine questions confirming
consensus: questions 1, 2, 3, 5, 6, 7, 9, 12, and 13. Besides the
aforementioned definitions for change management and competitive
advantage, the data revealed the Delphi panel has experienced
significant change in their organizations, each related to economic
conditions. For instance, in question 2, participants indicated they have
experienced significantly reduced revenue and margins, downsizing in
head count and expenses, and increased workloads for fewer
employees. The participants confirmed the precipitous nature of these

changes in question three by identifying the general economic environment, an increasingly competitive bid market, bank lending practices, and financial market instability. The Delphi panel also identified 10 change forces facing the U.S. metal building industry in the next five to 10 years, and 14 change forces facing the industry in the next 25 years.

The change forces represent a melding of ideas from a group of experienced leaders in the U.S. metal building industry, and signal the significance of forthcoming change perceived by the leaders. Perhaps more important, the change forces support study themes such as the need to constantly adapt, and the presence of economic conditions that force tough decisions. The change forces identified also show the forward thinking capabilities of the panel, and the ease of analyzing the responses in round two when the emergent list displayed remarkable similarity in responses. This trait points to a common understanding about future challenges facing the U.S. metal building industry. Lastly, the change forces represent an opportunity for future scholarly study through analysis of how the leaders manage the future change forces.

The change forces identified for the next five to 10 years included:

- Availability of capital;

- Availability of skilled labor;

- Energy codes;

- Government policies including market manipulation, and tax laws;

- Industry consolidation;

- Rapidly changing steel market;

- Raw material costs versus alternatives;

- Rebirth of competitive bid market and the lack of negotiated work;

- Unstable domestic economy; and

- Varied building design evident throughout industry.

The change forces identified for the next 25 years included the latter change forces, and (a) foreign competition, (b) increase in alternative construction methods and products, (c) new technology, and (d) shrinking consumer base because of baby boomer retirement.

These change forces were added to round three questions 5 and 6 in a multiple-choice format, and participants were asked to identify the top three in their opinion. In all questions except 5, 9, and 13, participants met consensus on three or fewer answers; these questions achieved four consensus answers. For round two data results, please see Appendix G.

Round three finalized the research study and revealed consensus for the remaining six questions: 4, 8, 10, 11, 14, and 15 (see Appendix H). In question 4, participants were asked how they recognize or forecast change forces. The analysis revealed participants focus on using (a) word of mouth information from suppliers and customers, (b) economic indicators, and (c) monitoring customers' buying behaviors and concerns. This data suggest the participants value internal and external sources for identifying potential change. In question 11, participants confirmed their belief that change forces can positively or negatively influence their organizations' ability to compete in the marketplace. Participants identified three specific areas including that change forces create a heightened awareness of organizational capabilities and value-added services for customers. This suggests the leaders see the change forces as integral to monitoring and adjusting organizational resources and an important concept for companies working in the 21st century global economy.

Participant data in round three also revealed consensus for questions 14 and 15, in which participants were asked to identify specific change forces facing the U.S. metal building industry. In question 14, participants identified (a) the availability of capital, (b) energy codes, and (c) government policies including market manipulation and tax laws as the greatest changes forces facing the industry in the next five to 10 years. Long-term, the participants identified government policies as the greatest change force facing the industry in the next 25 years. The answers to questions 14 and 15 suggest a belief among the leaders that the government, through its ability to regulate and tax, may create significant change influencing the industry in the short and long term.

Overall, the research study produced tangible results in three rounds. This confirmed the validity of the Delphi technique and the use of an expert panel to identify expert opinion on a topic with unknown answers. The data and findings also support the theory underpinning this study, systems theory. The interconnectedness of the world is evident throughout participant responses and the identification of internal and external change forces that influence their organizations. Research data suggests the panel participants do value change management, are conscious of internal and external change forces when creating strategy, and recognize the relationship of change management to competitive advantage.

In addition, the study represented an opportunity to explore an uncharted area in the U.S. metal building industry: change management methods and strategies. No studies in this area are known to exist for the industry. This study creates a new precedent for the industry by establishing a credible benchmark for existing and future industry leaders. The data gathered also add to the existing body of data on change management and provide the basis for future research in not only the U.S. metal building industry but also industry in general and the academic community.

Study Limitations

Shank (2006) described qualitative research "as a systematic empirical inquiry into meaning" (p. 6). This definition suggests a subjective influence when conducting a qualitative research study. Qualitative research is about more than numbers; it is about seeking answers to questions that may not fit into the stereotypical research study (Salkind, 2003) and trying to gain a better understanding of the subject matter (Shank, 2006). Because the literature revealed no data pertaining to change management strategies and methods used by leaders in the U.S. metal building industry, the study did not fit into previous research models and represented an opportunity to explore an unknown. A descriptive qualitative study using a questionnaire design was determined to be the most appropriate format to gather the data.

This research study was subject to limitations, including those inherent in qualitative research. Dobrovolny and Fuentes (2008) identified the following limitations inherent in qualitative research: (a) data analysis can be challenging, (b) time constraints to conduct the study, and (c) the availability of resources. Generalizability or being able to apply the data gathered from the research sample to a larger population is another important challenge for qualitative researchers (Shank, 2006). The potential for recreating the study for future research is also a concern.

The study followed the Delphi technique, using an expert panel to gather questionnaire data. The Delphi technique creates unique study limitations, the most important of which happens when conducting thematic analysis of data. Thematic analysis creates an opportunity for researcher bias because the researcher interprets the data. Mitigating this important limitation meant establishing a definition of consensus for this study to reduce the potential for the researcher to introduce any bias into the data analysis. For the purpose of this study, consensus was defined as any question on which at least 50% of participants show agreement.

This research study was subject to the following limitations because of the qualitative survey design and the Delphi technique:

1. The availability of a sample population: The study used a sample taken from a population of senior executives in the U.S. metal building industry. Although 141 organizations were identified, after exclusions only 64 organizations remained. From these organizations, 81 executives meeting participant criteria were identified.

2. The method for identifying the population and resulting sample: Although reliable industry sources, the Metal Building Manufacturers Association (MBMA) and the 2010 Metal Construction News (MCN) Metal Directory and Resource Guide, qualified candidates may have been excluded because their organizational data was not included.

3. Time constraints: The study used a sample of senior executives who because of their organizational role have limited time to commit to completing questionnaires. The round one questionnaire took an average of 20 minutes to complete, round two 18 minutes, and round three four minutes. Another consideration was the time the researcher could commit to the study, potentially limiting the time allotted to gathering data.

4. The Internet-based instrument delivery platform: QuestionPro created potential limitations when gathering data. The inability of study participants to review answers at any stage of a particular questionnaire may have hindered data collection since most survey questions are related to each other.

5. Three rounds may be inadequate for some studies: This study, like most Delphi studies, was completed in three rounds, with consensus determined on 60% of questions after round two. Consensus was determined on the remaining six questions during round three.

6. Current financial climate: The current economic environment may have unjustly influenced the responses to various questions such as the change forces identified by the Delphi panel.

Implications on Leadership

Change and why it happens has intrigued man for thousands of years. Early philosophers and scientists such as Socrates, Aristotle, and Bacon laid the groundwork for the anticipatory sciences (Joseph, 2007). The 19th and 20th centuries heralded new insights into the field of change management and new theories such as systems thinking. These new ways of thinking helped create a demand for organizational synergies and a need to involve the entire organization, including the external environment, in the decision-making process. This further promotes the field of change management. Perhaps the strongest precipitator of change management sciences has been the rapid pace of technological advances.

In the 21st century, technology is placing high demands on leaders to make faster and better decisions. Murray and Greenes (2006) described this phenomenon as adjusting to a flat global environment, and McLean (2007) as the plight of the boundary-less organization. An important construct for leaders in the decision-making process is knowledge, such as understanding why change happens and how to create a company that can adapt quickly. Leaders, by creating a flexible organization, may create a competitive advantage. Joroff, Porter, Feinberg, and Kukla (2003) stated this flexibility meant creating an agile organization. Agile organizations are dynamic and can readily transform to meet market demands (Joroff et al., 2003). This transformation supports the notion of the learning organization posited by Senge (2006). As the organization gains knowledge the organization implements the knowledge to deal with external change forces. This ability to transform or change may suggest a competitive advantage for the organization.

This research study's implications for leadership are significant not only for the U.S. metal building industry, but also for the business community at large, including the academic community. Change management is becoming critical for any organization. According to Arora (2003), research suggests "that 70 percent of all change initiatives fail or produce only middling results" (p. 43). This statement adds further value to the results of this research study and reemphasizes the importance of leaders becoming knowledgeable about change management, including how to implement change successfully in their organizations.

Charan (2009) confirmed this knowledge strategy by identifying six areas leaders should focus on to manage through tumultuous times such as those evident during the early 21st century: (a) being honest and exhibiting credibility to stakeholders, (b) finding ways to inspire team members, (c) maintaining a constant pulse on what is happening in the environment, (d) being realistic about goals while maintaining a strong vision, (e) getting involved in the operations— become a hands-on leader, and (f) keep planning for the future. These suggestions (Charan, 2009) point to the need for leaders to constantly look for ways to improve their organization in order to maintain or create a competitive advantage; monitoring change plays a significant role in this endeavor. Anthony and Christensen (2005) added that leaders who constantly scan the environment for potential change will become more knowledgeable and will gain the skills needed to adapt their organization to meet these future challenges. Change management represents an important leadership function for the modern global organization and an important construct of competitive advantage.

Murray and Greenes (2006) research supports the Charan (2009), and Anthony and Christensen (2005) arguments. Murray and Greenes (2006) identified four staples necessary to cope with future change: (a) leadership, (b) organization, (c) learning, and (d) technology. Each "pillar" described by Murray and Greenes (2006) suggests that organizational longevity and sustainable competitive advantage depends on the ability to learn and change in the organization (p. 358).

This study provided an opportunity to identify change management strategies and methods unique to the U.S. metal building industry. In particular, the study data identified new definitions for change management and competitive advantage and ways in which the leaders identify or forecast change and respond to change forces. These methods and strategies may apply to any industry and add to the knowledge available to leaders. The study results also create opportunities for future research by supporting a new model that leaders may use to identify and manage change in their organization. The *first-to-change mover advantage triangle* (FCMA) (see *Figure 1*) is based on the study research sub-questions:

1. How do leaders in the U.S. metal building industry perceive change management and identify, recognize, and differentiate between internal and external change forces?

2. How do leaders in the U.S. metal building industry respond to internal and external change, and how do these forces affect their change management strategies?

3. How do leaders in the U.S. metal building industry define competitive advantage, and how does change management influence creating a competitive advantage?

4. How do responses of leaders in the U.S. metal building industry reflect systems thinking, and what theories outlined in the conceptual or theoretical framework do their responses support?

The model melds the research data with the study sub-questions creating a synergistic framework for future scholarly study in the field of change management. Specifically the research data supports the model by providing suggestions to accomplish each step in the triangle. The data not only answers the research sub-questions, but also by incorporating the data into the model, creates a viable process map leaders may use to guide the change process in their respective organizations. Research sub-questions one, two, and three are shown in triangle building blocks a, b, c, and d. The final research sub-question is represented by the systems-like appearance of the triangle building blocks. Each building block depends on the other for support; if one block is out of place, the triangle would fail.

Each building block of the triangle shows evidence from the data results. Questions 1, 2, 3, and 4 of the research data correlate with building block a, and identified techniques for identifying and forecasting change including a definition of change management. Questions 5, 6, and 8 align with building block b providing insight into how the leaders differentiate between internal external change forces. Building block c is supported by study questions 7 and 9, describing how the leaders responded to the change forces. Building block d corresponds to questions 10, 11, 12, and 13 and confirmed the perceived importance of change management on organizational competitive advantage. The relationship is obvious throughout the research data, confirming the model support. Although the model is supported by data gathered from leaders in U.S. metal building industry, the model identifies a process leaders in any industry may use to manage change. The model also creates opportunity for future scholarly research in the field of change management.

The FCMA triangle suggests leaders may achieve a first-to-change mover advantage for their organizations by:

1. Developing strategies to identify and forecast change by using economic indicators, word-of-mouth data from suppliers and vendors, and monitoring customer buying behaviors;

2. Differentiating between internal and external forces so that strategies may be unique based on the change force origin;

3. Developing a response to the change forces such as redistributing responsibilities, increasing communication in organization, and identifying new products and services to meet the change forces and help the organization maintain an edge; and

4. Using the change forces to create a competitive advantage by demanding constant organizational improvement and identifying ways to constantly adapt to meet stakeholder needs.

The FCMA Triangle

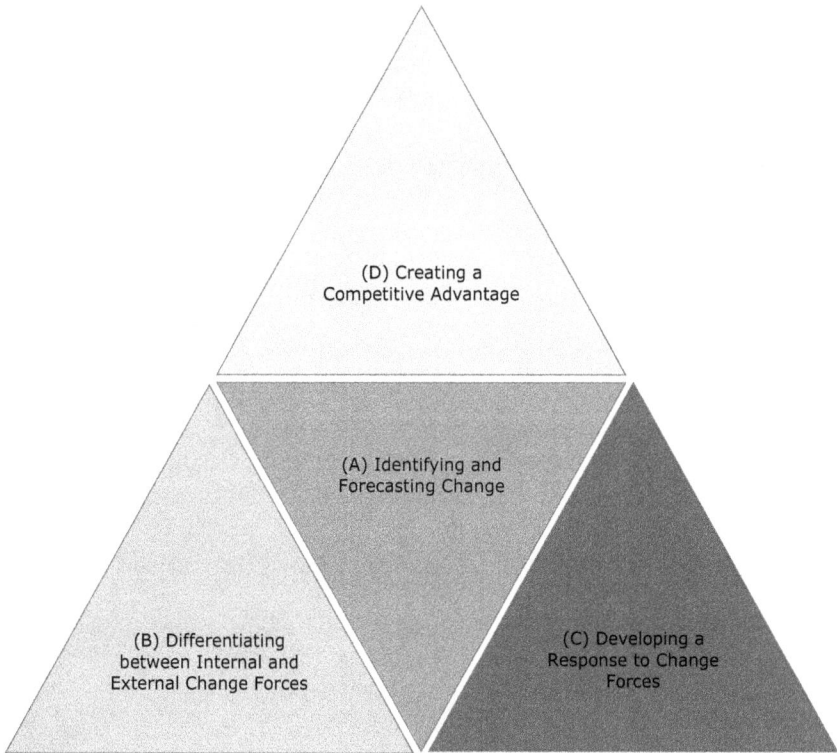

Figure 1. Shows the First-to-Change Mover Advantage triangle (FCMA).

Conclusions

The research study represents a milestone for leaders in the U.S. metal building industry because the study may be the first time industry leaders have come together to study issues related to change management. This unique accomplishment establishes a new benchmark for U.S. metal building industry leaders by creating a knowledge base to build on; it supports previous studies done in other fields about change management methods and strategies. Evidence of this knowledge base comes from the FCMA model (See *Figure 1*) and the assertions that organizations may gain a distinct competitive advantage based on the leader's ability to identify and manage change in advance of competitors. The long-term value of the study is evident for leaders of the U.S. metal building industry, other industries, and the academic community.

Recommendations for Future Research

Change management is a rich and broad field, with applicability to any organization in any industry. This research study has created opportunity for future research in the area of change management strategies and methods related not only to the U.S. metal building industry but also to industry in general. Possible future research may include:

1. Performing a similar study in a related or unrelated industry and comparing and contrasting the results to determine variances in industry change management techniques. This also may help identify new management strategies and methods.

2. Extending the study to global markets in the metal building industry to determine if change management

strategies and methods vary by location, such as country location. This also may identify new change forces and develop a broader understanding of the change forces facing the industry at large.

3. Creating a study to examine the short and long-term change forces identified by the panel.

4. Expanding the study to include non-senior executives and managers in organizations. This may add a depth of insight not evident in the original study.

5. Testing or applying the FCMA model to organizations in the U.S. metal building industry and beyond. This may further confirm the model, identify needed changes to the model design, and build on this study's research in the field of change management.

Perhaps the most important opportunity for future study comes in the form of how the present study data may be interpreted to develop new change management strategies for the U.S. metal building industry. For instance, the literature is rich with change management data, but no data exists for the U.S. metal building industry. This study potentially represents the first such study to ever be conducted about the U.S. metal building industry. Because of this, the study has provided significant opportunity for future learning and growth not only from the existing data, but also through future interpretation of the data.

Drucker (1999) declared that leaders in the 21st century will "face long years of profound changes" (p. 92). This statement points to the need for leaders to recognize and learn to manage and prepare for change. How leaders in the U.S. metal building industry identify, manage, and prepare their organizations for change is critical at the organizational level, and at the industry level to ensure future competitive advantage. The global economy present in the 21st century is creating the need for all business leaders to be cognizant and knowledgeable of change and change forces. An example of these forces is evident in the availability of alternative building products because of global competitors in industries competing for construction dollars. Understanding how to manage these change forces may determine an organization's and industries long-term success.

Recommendation for Higher Education

Another aspect of this research study is the implications for higher education and learning. The importance of teaching students the relationship of change management and competitive advantage centers on the ability to use study data such as the *first-to-change mover advantage triangle* in the classroom. Schein (1999) described this as "cognitive restructuring," in which individuals use new insights to broaden and change their assumptions (p. 61). Developing a case study based on study data may satisfy this need, by providing an instrument educators can use in the classroom. Case studies provide a focused approach to studying a subject and creating dialogue in group discussions (Salkind, 2003). Such discussions may reveal new areas for future study, including insight into the theoretical basis. Overall, the applicability of the study in the classroom is rich. The case study approach may be the optimal means to move the study into the classroom.

Summary

Understanding how to identify, forecast, manage, and promote change is critical for leaders in the 21st century global economy. For leaders to succeed in today's ultra-competitive markets requires leaders to develop a knowledge base and willingness to learn and constantly adapt. These requirements extend to the organization, placing the burden on the organizational leaders to create a culture that includes policies promoting change and adaptation. This research study revealed a framework containing specific suggestions for leaders: (a) identify change forces that exist in the environment, (b) establish the capabilities to distinguish between internal and external change forces, (c) develop strategies to manage the change forces, and (d) use the change forces to create a sustainable competitive advantage. These suggestions align with other research in the field of change

management, such as theory zyx, in which Arora (2003) outlined a

change management framework: planning (z-axis), execution (y-axis),

and people (x-axis). Holland (2000) argued for leaders to develop ways

to (a) understand change, (b) lead change, (c) engineer change, (d)

manage change, and (e) master change. The FCMA triangle aligns with

the Holland (2000) suggestions further validating the model.

The research data also provided short-term and long-term

views of change forces facing the U.S. metal building industry. The

change forces create a unique but broad perspective that, like the

FCMA triangle, may apply to any industry. Forces identified included

(a) availability of capital, (b) energy codes, and (c) government policies.

The forces suggest the industry is subject to influence from a range of

sources, the most important of which may come from government

policies including regulations and taxation. By acknowledging these

potential future change forces, U.S. metal building industry leaders may

be able to establish policies and strategies internally and externally for

their organizations to successfully manage these changes. This

proactive stance on change management may be the link to becoming a

leader of change at the organization and industry level.

This research study reaffirms the call throughout the literature

review for a holistic or systems-based perspective when leading an organization. This applies to how leaders manage change and create organizations adaptable to quickly changing environments. The research also points to a need for leaders to become proactive and lead change rather than taking a secondary or reactive role, suggesting a manager's perspective. The axiom that leaders create change (Landale, 2004) fits the research intent, helping leaders become change leaders in their respective organizations and industries.

The benefits of this research study are yet unproven, but what is known is the study has created an expanded perspective on change management strategies and methods applicable to any industry. The study represents a benchmark for existing and future leaders in the U.S. metal building industry to gauge their change knowledge and policies. The study created a long-term framework that leaders in any industry may use to establish, enhance, or guide their ability to lead change.

Personal Reflection

This research study has been a personal journey in which as a learner and working professional I have grown immensely. Perhaps the most significant take-away from conducting this study was the revelation that leaders in the U.S. metal building industry have a strong, almost innate desire to use change to create a competitive advantage for their organizations. The study data suggests the leaders not only understand the implications of change on their organizations, but also the need to evolve to meet market demands in the new global economy. Because of my nearly 16 years of sales and management experience in the U.S. metal building industry, I entered the study with assumptions, such as questioning the ability and desire of industry leaders to recognize and use change. I am leaving the study with new perceptions of U.S. metal building industry leaders and a strong desire to further develop and use study data not only to promote change knowledge in the industry, but in academe as well. I am excited about what the future holds.

References

Aaron, S. (2010). Sustainability: Harnessing the collective innovation of all employees. *People and Strategy, 33*(1), 14. Retrieved from http://proquest.umi.com/pqdweb?did=2024554861&Fmt=7 &clientId=13118&RQT=309&VName=PQD

Abella, A. (2008). *Soldiers of reason: The RAND corporation and the rise of the American empire*: New York, NY: Mariner Books.

Adcroft, A., Willis, R., & Hurst, J. (2008). A new model for managing change: the holistic view. *The Journal of Business Strategy, 29*(1), 40. doi:10.1108/02756660810845697

Aitken, S., & Morgan, J. (1999). How Motorola promotes good health. *The Journal for Quality and Participation, 22*(1), 54. Retrieved from http://proquest.umi.com/pqdweb?did=38510247&Fmt=7&cl ientId=13118&RQT=309&VName=PQD

Alaa, G. (2009). Derivation of factors facilitating organizational emergence based on complex adaptive systems and social autopoiesis theories. *Emergence: Complexity and Organization, 11*(1), 19. Retrieved from http://nexttoppersonalgrowthauthor.info/ECO/submitted_m anuscripts.aspx?AspxAutoDetectCookieSupport=1

Alsaaty, F., & Harris, M. (2009). The innovation event: An insight into the occurrence of innovation. *The business review, Cambridge, 14*(1), 292. Retrieved from http://proquest.umi.com/pqdweb?did=1921041861&Fmt=7&clientId=13118&RQT=309&VName=PQD

Anonymous (Ed.) (1996) *Webster's II new riverside dictionary*. Boston, MA: Houghton Mifflin Company.

Anthony, S. A., & Christensen, C. M. (2005). How You Can Benefit By Predicting Change. *Financial Executive, 21*(2), 36-41. Retrieved from http://search.ebscohost.com/login.aspx?direct=true&db=bth&AN=16284823&site=ehost-live

Arora, N. (2003). *Theory zyx of successful change management: A definitive practical guide to reach the next level*. Gardena, CA: L.A. Press.

Beitler, M. A. (2006). *Strategic organizational change: A practitioner's guide for managers and consultants* (2nd ed.). Greensboro, NC: Practitioner Press International.

Billick, B., & Peterson, J. A. (2001). *Competitive leadership: Twelve principles for success*. Chicago, IL: Triumph Books.

Borrego, M., Douglas, E., & Amelink, C. (2009). Quantitative,

qualitative, and mixed research methods in engineering

education. *Journal of Engineering Education, 98*(1), 53. Retrieved

from

http://proquest.umi.com/pqdweb?did=1850875531&Fmt=7

&clientId=2606&RQT=309&VName=PQD

Boulding, K. E. (1956). General systems theory—The skeleton of

science. *Management Science, 2*(3), 197-208.

doi:10.1287/mnsc.2.3.197

Boyatzis, R. E. (2006). An overview of intentional change from a

complexity perspective. *The Journal of Management Development,

25*(7), 607. doi:10.1108/02621710610678445

Boyatzis, R. E., & Akrivou, K. (2006). The ideal self as the driver of

intentional change. *The Journal of Management Development, 25*(7),

624. doi:10.1108/02621710610678454

Boyatzis, R., & McKee, A. (2006). Intentional change. *Journal of

Organizational Excellence.* doi:10.1002/joe.20100

Burlando, T. (1994). Chaos and risk management. *Risk Management,

41*(4), 54. Retrieved from

http://proquest.umi.com/pqdweb?did=772137&Fmt=7&clien

tId=13118&RQT=309&VName=PQD

Bussolari, C., & Goodell, J. (2009). Chaos theory as a model for life

transitions counseling: Nonlinear dynamics and life's changes.

Journal of Counseling and Development: JCD, 87(1), 98. Retrieved

from

http://aca.metapress.com/openurl.asp?genre=article&issn=07

48-9633&volume=87&issue=1&spage=98

Carter, E. (2008). Successful change requires more than change

management. *The Journal for Quality and Participation, 31*(1), 20.

Retrieved from

http://asq.org/pub/jqp/past/2008/spring/index.html

Cassell, C., Symon, G., Buehring, A., & Johnson, P. (2006). The role

and status of qualitative methods in management research: an

empirical account. *Management Decision, 44*(2), 290-290-303. doi:

10.1108/00251740610650256

Charan, R. (2009). *Leadership in the era of economic uncertainty*. New York,

NY: McGraw-Hill.

Chen, C.-A. (2008). Linking the knowledge creation process to

organizational theories. *Journal of Organizational Change

Management, 21*(3), 259. doi:10.1108/09534810810874778

Christensen, C. M. (2006). *The innovator's dilemma*. New York, NY:

Collins Business Essentials.

Christensen, H. K. (2010). Defining customer value as the driver of

competitive advantage. *Strategy & Leadership, 38*(5), 20.

doi:10.1108/10878571011072048

Christensen, C., & Mangelsdorf, M. (2009). Good days for disruptors.

MIT Sloan Management Review, 50(3), 67. Retrieved from

http://sloanreview.mit.edu/files/saleable-pdfs/50314.pdf

Coghlan, D., & Brannick, T. (2003). Kurt Lewin: The "practical

theorist" for the twenty-first century. *Irish Journal of Management,

24*(2), 31. Retrieved from

http://www.iamireland.com/index.html

Cohen, W. A. (2008). *A class with Drucker.* New York, NY: AMACOM.

Comeau-Kirschner, C., & Wah, L. (1999). Holistic management.

Management Review, 88(11), 26. Retrieved from

http://proquest.umi.com/pqdweb?did=46827627&Fmt=7&cl

ientId=13118&RQT=309&VName=PQD

Cope, J. (2009). Adapt to survive and thrive. *The British Journal of

Administrative Management,* 26. Retrieved from

http://search.proquest.com/docview/224609048?accountid=3

5812

Creswell, J. W. (1994). *Research design: Qualitative and quantitative

approaches.* Thousand Oaks, CA: Sage Publications.

Dalkey, N., & Helmer, O. (1963). An experimental application of the

   Delphi method to the use of experts. *Management Science (pre-*

   1986), 9(3), 458. doi:10.1287/mnsc.9.3.458

Delen, D., & Al-Hawamdeh, S. (2009). A holistic framework for

   knowledge discovery and management. *Communications of the*

   ACM, 52(6), 141-145. doi:10.1145/1516046.1516082

Demers, C. (2007). *Organizational change theories: A synthesis.* Los Angeles:

   Sage Publications.

Dengler, R. A. (2006). *Fast-acting OD intervention for expedited organization*

   culture change: A quantitative evaluation of a field experiment in a large

   utility undergoing an intentionally violent transformational change.

   Unpublished doctoral dissertation, Benedictine University,

   Springfield, Illinois. Retrieved from

   http://proquest.umi.com/pqdweb?did=1051279231&Fmt=7

   &clientId=2606&RQT=309&VName=PQD

Diderot, D. (1755/2002). Encyclopédie (P. Stewart, Trans.) (Vol. 5, pp.

   635-648A). Retrieved from

   http://quod.lib.umich.edu/cgi/t/text/text-

   idx?c=did;cc=did;rgn=main;view=text;idno=did2222.0000.004

Dobrovolny, J., & Fuentes, S. (2008). Quantitative versus qualitative

   evaluation: A tool to decide which to use. *Performance*

   Improvement, 47(4), 7. doi:10.1002/pfi.197

Drucker, P. F. (1999). *Management challenges for the 21st century*. New York, NY: Harper Business.

Fodness, D. (2005). Rethinking strategic marketing: achieving breakthrough results. *The Journal of Business Strategy, 26*(3), 20. doi:10.1108/02756660510597074

Furrer, O., Sudharshan, D., Thomas, H., & Alexandre, M. T. (2008). Resource configurations, generic strategies, and firm performance. *Journal of Strategy and Management, 1*(1), 15. doi:10.1108/17554250810909400

Gabb, J., Balen, R., Gibbs, G., Hall, C., & Teal, A. (2006). Victoria climbié inquiry data Corpus project: Using the Delphi method in multidisciplinary child protection research. *British Journal of Social Work, 36*(4), 577. doi:10.1093/bjsw/bch303

Galagan, P. (2010). Bridging the skills gap: Part II. *Public Manager, 39*(2), 52. Retrieved from http://www.thepublicmanager.org/docs_articles/current/Vol 39,2010/Vol39,Issue02/Vol39N2_BridgingSkillsGap_Galagan. pdf

Galán, J., Monje, J., & Zúñiga-Vicente, J. (2009). Implementing change

in smaller firms. *Research Technology Management, 52*(1), 59.

Retrieved from

http://search.ebscohost.com.ezproxy.apollolibrary.com/login.

aspx?direct=true&db=bth&AN=36382257&site=ehost-live

Garland, E. (2007). Getting ahead by looking ahead. *The Futurist* (July-

August). Retrieved from

http://search.ebscohost.com.ezproxy.apollolibrary.com/login.

aspx?direct=true&db=a9h&AN=25310551&site=ehost-live

Gonnering, S. R. (2010). The future demands complex leadership (On

the Edge of Chaos: Leadership Theory). *Physician Executive, 36*,

6. Retrieved from

http://search.ebscohost.com.ezproxy.apollolibrary.com/login.

aspx?direct=true&db=bth&AN=48364918&site=ehost-live

Grisham, T. (2009). The Delphi technique: a method for testing

complex and multifaceted topics. *International Journal of Managing

Projects in Business, 2*(1), 112. doi:10.1108/17538370910930545

Hamel, G. (2000). *Leading the revolution.* Boston, MA: Harvard Business

School Press.

Hamel, G., & Prahalad, C. K. (1994). *Competing for the future.* Boston,

MA: Harvard Business School Press.

Hammer, M. (2004). Deep change. *Harvard Business Review, 82*(4), 84-93.

Retrieved from

http://search.ebscohost.com/login.aspx?direct=true&db=bth
&AN=12774666&site=ehost-live

Harper, S. C., & Glew, D. J. (2008). Becoming an ever-evolving

enterprise. *Industrial Management, 50*(3), 22. Retrieved from

http://search.ebscohost.com/login.aspx?direct=true&db=f5h
&AN=32613490&site=ehost-live

Helmer, O. (1972). Prospects of technological progress. In A. Toffler

(Ed.), *The futurists*. New York, NY: Random House.

Holland, W. E. (2000). *Change is the rule: Practical actions for change on time,*

on target, on budget. Chicago, IL: Dearborn.

Hostetler, D. (2010). Get results: Improve your accounting firm

processes using Lean Six Sigma. *Journal of Accountancy, 209*(1),

38. Retrieved from

http://www.journalofaccountancy.com/Issues/2010/Jan/200
91484

Howard, A. (2006). Positive and negative emotional attractors and

intentional change. *The Journal of Management Development, 25*(7),

657. doi:10.1108/02621710610678472

Hwang, J., & Christensen, C. (2008). Disruptive innovation in health
    care delivery: A framework for business-model innovation.
    Health Affairs, 27(5), 1329. doi:10.1377/hlthaff.27.5.1329

Johnson, R. A., Kast, F. E., & Rosenzweig, J. E. (1964). Systems theory
    and management. *Management Science, 10*(2), 367-384.
    doi:10.1287/mnsc.10.2.387

Joroff, M. L., Porter, W. L., Feinberg, B., & Kukla, C. (2003). The agile
    workplace. *Journal of Corporate Real Estate, 5*(4), 293.
    doi:10.1108/14630010310812145

Joseph, E. (2007). Discovering the anticipatory sciences. *Futurics,
    31*(3/4), 2. Retrieved from

    http://search.proquest.com.ezproxy.apollolibrary.com/docvie
    w/219811403?accountid=35812

Karp, T. (2006). Transforming organisations for organic growth: The
    DNA of change leadership. *Journal of Change Management, 6*(1),
    3-20. doi:10.1080/14697010600565186

Knab, E. (2008). *Going global: Success factors for penetrating emerging markets.*
    Unpublished Doctoral Dissertation, University of Phoenix,
    www.phoenix.edu. Retrieved from

    http://proquest.umi.com/pqdweb?did=1597603391&Fmt=7
    &clientId=2606&RQT=309&VName=PQD

Kuhfittig, P. K. F., & Davis, T. W. (1990). Predicting the unpredictable.

Cost Engineering, 32(2), 7. Retrieved from

http://search.proquest.com.ezproxy.apollolibrary.com/docvie

w/220433571?accountid=35812

Landale, A. (2004). Being a leader of change. *The British Journal of*

Administrative Management, 18. Retrieved from

http://search.proquest.com/docview/224615306?accountid=3

5812

Leong, L., & Jarmoszko, A. (2010). Analyzing capabilities and

enterprise strategy: A value proposition framework. *International*

Journal of Management and Information Systems, 14(1), 53. Retrieved

from

http://search.proquest.com.ezproxy.apollolibrary.com/docvie

w/195294189?accountid=35812

Lönnqvist, A., Sillanpää, V., & Kianto, A. (2009). Using intellectual

capital management for facilitating organizational change.

Journal of Intellectual Capital, 10(4), 559.

doi:10.1108/14691930910996643

Low, J., & Kalafut, P. C. (2002). *Invisible advantage: How intangibles are*

driving business performance. Cambridge, MA: Perseus Publishing.

Lucia, Ş. G. (2008). Innovation - Source to obtain the competitive

advantage in the global economy. *Annals of the University of

Oradea, Economic Science Series, 17*(2), 767-771. Retrieved from

http://search.ebscohost.com/login.aspx?direct=true&db=bth

&AN=48129360&site=ehost-live

Maccoby, M. (2010). Learn change leadership from two great teachers.

Research Technology Management, 53(2), 68. Retrieved from

http://search.proquest.com.ezproxy.apollolibrary.com/docvie

w/213802286?accountid=35812

Mann , J. (2010). Futurists vs. planners: Given the rapid speed of

business today, forward-thinking companies should consider

futurology to stay ahead of change. *The Futurist, 36*, 68.

Retrieved from

http://go.galegroup.com.ezproxy.apollolibrary.com/ps/i.do?id

=GALE%7CA90333412&v=2.1&u=uphoenix&it=r&p=GPS

&sw=w

McAneny, P. J. (2010). Red is good: Transformational changes for Air

Force aircraft maintenance. *Air Force Journal of Logistics, 34*(1/2),

120. Retrieved from

http://www.aflma.hq.af.mil/shared/media/document/AFD-

100505-028.pdf

McDonald, J. M. (2000). Managing rapid change: From theory to

    practice: An invited article. *Southern Business Review, 25*(2), 28.

    Retrieved from

    http://coba.georgiasouthern.edu/centers/pub/Southern%20B

    usiness%20Review/spring2000/Michael%20McDonald.htm

McGrath, R., & MacMillan, I. (2009). How to rethink your business

    during uncertainty. *MIT Sloan Management Review, 50*(3), 25.

    Retrieved from http://sloanreview.mit.edu/the-

    magazine/2009-spring/50308/how-to-rethink-your-business-

    during-uncertainty/

McLaughlin, S. (2009). The imperatives of e-business: case study of a

    failed project. *The Journal of Business Strategy, 30*(1), 40.

    doi:10.1108/02756660910926966

McLean, J. (2007). Prepare for the future. It's happening fast! *The British

    Journal of Administrative Management*, 17. Retrieved from

    http://proquest.umi.com/pqdweb?did=1274354351&Fmt=7

    &clientId=13118&RQT=309&VName=PQD

Meadows, D. H. (2008). *Thinking in systems: A primer.* White River

    Junction, Vermont: Chelsea Green Publishing.

Mockler, R. J. (1968). The systems approach to business organization and decision making. *California Management Review, 11*(2), 53-58. Retrieved from

http://search.ebscohost.com/login.aspx?direct=true&db=bth&AN=5049242&site=ehost-live

Moore, G. A. (2005). *Dealing with Darwin: How great companies innovate at every phase of their evolution.* New York, NY: Penguin Books.

Morabito, J., Sack, I., Stohr, E., & Bhate, A. (2009). Designing flexible organizations. *Global Journal of Flexible Systems Management, 10*(2), 1. Retrieved from

http://search.proquest.com.ezproxy.apollolibrary.com/docview/201695035?accountid=35812

Mueller, J. (2009). Maxims of maximizing organizational change effectiveness. *The Business Review, Cambridge, 14*(1), 70. Retrieved from

http://search.proquest.com.ezproxy.apollolibrary.com/docview/197310537?accountid=35812

Mulej, M., Potocan, V., Zenko, Z., Kajzer, S., et al. (2004). How to restore Bertalanffian systems thinking. *Kybernetes, 33*(1), 48. doi:10.1108/03684920410514346

Mullen, P. M. (2003). Delphi: Myths and reality. *Journal of Health Organization and Management, 17*(1), 37. doi:10.1108/14777260310469319

Murray, A. J., & Greenes, K. A. (2006). New leadership strategies for the enterprise of the future. *VINE, 36*(4), 358. doi:10.1108/03055720610716629

Newman, J. (2009). Building a creative high-performance R&D culture. *Research Technology Management, 52*(5), 21. Retrieved from http://search.proquest.com.ezproxy.apollolibrary.com/docvie w/213799772?accountid=35812

Newstrom, J. W., & Davis, K. (2002). *Organizational behavior* (11th ed.). New York, NY: McGraw-Hill Higher Education.

Nichols, R. W. (1999). The futures business. *Sciences, 39*(5), 4. Retrieved from http://www.nyas.org/Publications/Default.aspx

Norbutus, D. (2007). *Exploring the experience of organizational transformation: Contrasting episodic change with continuous change.* Unpublished doctoral dissertation, Regent University, Virginia Beach, VA. Retrieved from http://proquest.umi.com/pqdweb?did=1453181031&Fmt=7 &clientId=2606&RQT=309&VName=PQD

Norton, D. W., & II, B. J. P. (2009). Unique experiences: Disruptive innovations offer customers more "time well spent." *Strategy & Leadership, 37*(6), 4. doi:10.1108/10878570911001435

Olavarrieta, S., & Ellinger, A. E. (1997). Resource-based theory and strategic logistics research. *International Journal of Physical Distribution & Logistics Management, 27*(9/10), 559. doi:10.1108/09600039710188594

Oosten, E. B. V. (2006). Intentional change theory at the organizational level: a case study. *The Journal of Management Development, 25*(7), 707. doi:10.1108/02621710610678508

Padel, S., & Midmore, P. (2005). The development of the European market for organic products: insights from a Delphi study. *British Food Journal, 107*(8), 626. doi:10.1108/00070700510611011

Pellettiere, V. (2006). Organization self-assessment to determine the readiness and risk for a planned change. *Organization Development Journal, 24*(4), 38. Retrieved from http://search.proquest.com.ezproxy.apollolibrary.com/docvie w/197977810?accountid=35812

Phillips, J. J. (2005). *Investing in your company's human capital: Strategies to avoid spending too little or too much.* New York, NY: AMACOM.

Plant, T. (2008). Holistic strategic planning: Achieving sustainable

results. *Public Management (00333611), 90*(10), 17. Retrieved

from

http://search.proquest.com.ezproxy.apollolibrary.com/docvie

w/204189732?accountid=35812

Porter, M. E. (1985). *Competitive advantage: Creating and sustaining superior

performance*. New York, NY: The Free Press.

Powell, C. (2003). The Delphi technique: myths and realities. *Journal of

Advanced Nursing, 41*(4), 376-382.

doi:10.1046/j.1365-2648.2003.02537.x

Resnicow, K. P., & Page, S. P. (2008). Embracing chaos and

complexity: A quantum change for public health. *American

Journal of Public Health, 98*(8), 1382.

doi:10.2105/AJPH.2007.129460

Rosenberg, D. (2003). Early modern information overload. *Journal of the

History of Ideas, 64*(1), 1. doi:10.1353/jhi.2003.0017

Salkind, N. (2003). *Exploring research* (5th ed.). Upper Saddle River, NJ:

Prentice Hall.

Schein, E. H. (1999). Kurt Lewin's change theory in the field and in the

classroom: Notes toward a model of managed learning.

[Article]. *Reflections, 1*(1), 59-74. doi:10.1162/152417399570287

Schenck, E. (2007). *The Houdini solution: Put creativity and innovation to work by thinking inside the box*. New York, NY: McGraw-Hill.

Senge, P. M. (2006). *The fifth discipline: the art and practice of a learning organization*. New York, NY: Doubleday.

Shank, G. D. (2006). *Qualitative research: A personal skills approach* (2nd ed.). Upper Saddle River, NJ: Pearson Merrill.

Sharp, M. (2010). Development of an instrument to measure students' perceptions of information technology fluency skills: Establishing content validity. *Perspectives in Health Information Management*, 1. Retrieved from http://proquest.umi.com/pqdweb?did=2118694901&Fmt=7&clientId=13118&RQT=309&VName=PQD

Sheehan, N. T., & Foss, N. J. (2009). Exploring the roots of Porter's activity-based view. *Journal of Strategy and Management, 2*(3), 240. doi:10.1108/17554250910982480

Stanley, G. (1999). Management and complex adaptation. *Management International, Vol. 3*(No 2), 69. Retrieved from http://managementinternational.ca/en/field-of-interests/management-general_en/page/12

Stebbins, L. (2010). Development of reality system theory. *Journal of Business & Economics Research, 8*(4), 1. Retrieved from http://search.proquest.com.ezproxy.apollolibrary.com/docvie w/194902471?accountid=35812

Taylor, S. N. (2006). Why the real self is fundamental to intentional change. *The Journal of Management Development, 25*(7), 643. doi:10.1108/02621710610678463

Teijlingen, E. v., & Hundley, V. (2002). The importance of pilot studies. *Nursing Standard, 16*(40), 33. Retrieved from http://search.proquest.com.ezproxy.apollolibrary.com/docvie w/219814873?accountid=35812

Tersine, R. J., & Riggs, W. E. (1976). The Delphi technique: A long-range planning tool. *Business Horizons, 19*(2), 51. doi:10.1016/0007-6813(76)90081-1

Theodore, T. K., & Bronson, L. (1987). Achieving competitive advantage: A holistic approach to management. *Management Review, 76*(6), 52. Retrieved from http://proquest.umi.com/pqdweb?did=640546&Fmt=7&clien tId=13118&RQT=309&VName=PQD

Toffler, A. (Ed.). (1972). *The futurists.* New York, NY: Random House.

Tsai, C.-F., & Yen, Y.-F. (2008). A model to explore the mystery

between organizations' downsizing strategies and firm

performance. *Journal of Organizational Change Management, 21*(3),

367. doi:10.1108/09534810810874831

Tucker, P. (2010). The science of "tipping points." *The Futurist, 44*(1), 6.

Retrieved from

http://proquest.umi.com/pqdweb?did=1923180151&Fmt=7

&clientId=13118&RQT=309&VName=PQD

Tuominen, K. (2000). *Managing change: Practical strategies for competitive*

advantage. Milwaukee, WI: ASQ.

Van Buren, H., III. (2008). Building relational wealth in the new

economy: How can firms leverage the value of organizational

social capital. *International Journal of Management, 25*(4), 684.

Retrieved from

http://proquest.umi.com/pqdweb?did=1623336601&Fmt=7

&clientId=13118&RQT=309&VName=PQD

Von Bertalanffy, L. (1972). The history and status of general systems

theory. *Academy of Management Journal, 15*(4), 407-426. Retrieved

from

http://search.ebscohost.com/login.aspx?direct=true&db=bth

&AN=4297533&site=ehost-live

Vorakulpipat, C., & Rezgui, Y. (2008). Value creation: the future of

knowledge management. *The Knowledge Engineering Review, 23*(3),

283. doi:10.1017/S0269888908001380

Walters, D., Halliday, M., & Glaser, S. (2002). Creating value in the

"new economy." *Management Decision, 40*(7/8), 775.

doi:10.1108/00251740210441027

Wright, S. (2010). Dealing with resistance. *Nursing Standard, 24*(23), 18.

Retrieved from

http://proquest.umi.com/pqdweb?did=1966408771&Fmt=7

&clientId=13118&RQT=309&VName=PQD

Yang, Y. (2009). An investigation of group interaction functioning

stimulated by transformational leadership on employee

intrinsic and extrinsic job satisfaction: An extension of the

resource-based theory perspective. *Social Behavior and Personality,

37*(9), 1259. doi:10.2224/sbp.2009.37.9.1259

Appendix A
List of Potential Organizations

MBMA Members:
A&S Building Systems, Inc.
ACI Building Systems, Inc.
Alliance Steel, Inc.
American Buildings Company
BC Steel Buildings
Behlen Building Systems
Bigbee Steel Buildings, Inc.
BlueScope Buildings North America, Inc.
Butler Manufacturing Company
CBC Steel Buildings
CECO Building Systems
Chief Buildings
Dean Steel Buildings, Inc.
Garco Building Systems, Inc.
Golden Giant, Inc.
Gulf States Manufacturers
HCI Steel Building Systems
Heritage Building Systems
Inland Buildings
Kirby Building Systems, Inc.
Liberty Building Systems, Inc.
Ludwig Buildings, Inc.
Mesco Building Solutions
Metallic Building Company
Mid-West Steel Buildings
NCI Building Systems, Inc.
Nucor Building Systems
Oakland Metal Buildings, Inc.
Package Industries, Inc.
Pinnacle Structures, Inc.
Red Dot Buildings
Ruffin Building Systems, Inc.
Schulte Building Systems, L.P.
Spirco Manufacturing
Star Building Systems
Steel Built Corporation
Trident Building Systems, Inc.
Tyler Building Systems, L.P.
United Structures of America, Inc.
Varco Pruden Buildings
Vulcan Steel Structures, Inc.
Whirlwind Steel Buildings

MCN Resource Guide*:
A&D Building Systems, Inc.
Adel Steel, Inc.
Agate, Inc.
Albers Manufacturing Co., Inc.
American Pre-Fabricated Structures, Inc.
American Steel Building Co., Inc.
Anderson Steel, Inc.
Armor Steel Buildings, Inc.
Associated Metal Components, LLC.
ATY Building Systems, Inc.
Aviation Building Systems
Borga, Inc.
Bottomline Buildings, Inc.
Building Component Sales
Bulldog Building Systems, Inc.
Bunger Steel, Inc.
Carport Sales Co
Commander Buildings, Inc.
Components Plus, Inc.
Corle Building Systems, Inc.
Coronis Building Systems, Inc.
Corrugated Industries of Florida, Inc.
Crown Metal Buildings, Inc.
Custom Component & Building, Inc.
Custom Metal Building Product
Deluxe Building Systems
Diversified Hangar
EagleSpan Steel Structures, Inc.
EBC, Inc.
EPS Buildings
Essex Structural Steel Co., Inc.
Express Building Systems
Fast Trac Buildings, Inc.
Florida Pre-Fab, Inc.
Foremost Buildings, Inc.
Freedom Steel
GalvaBuild North America
GEM Buildings
Gold Seal Steel Buildings, Inc.
Gorilla Steel, LLC
Henry Building Systems
Ironbuilt Steel Buildings

Kodiak Steel Homes
Kustom Buildings, Inc.
Leslie Industries, Inc.
Liberty Steel
Lifetime Steel Buildings, Inc.
Magnatrax Corporation
Majestic Metals, Inc.
MD Enterprises, Inc.
Miller Building Systems, Inc.
Mueller, Inc.
Northern Building Systems
Northern Steel International
Nunno Corporation
O'Steel, Inc.
Olympia Steel Buildings
OSI Building Systems
Pacific Building Systems
Panel Steel Buildings, Inc.
Parkline, Inc.
Perfect Steel Systems
Perka Buildings
PorterCorp
Portland Systems
Progressive Steel Buildings
R&M Steel Company
R.L.S Structures, Inc.
Rabco Corporation
Repco Industries, Inc.
Rhino Steel Building Syst., Inc.
Rib Roof Metal Systems, Inc.
Rigid Building Systems
Rockford Mfr Ltd.
Sentinel Building Systems
Shenango Steel Buildings, Inc.
Southern Structures, Inc.
Southwind Building Systems
Space Buildings
Standard Structures, Inc.
Statewide Steel, Inc.
Steel Building Fabricators
Steel Service Building Co.
STEELBUILDING.COM
Steelbuildingsupplier.com
SteelMaster Buildings

*Duplicates removed

MCN Resource Guide*, Cont.:
Steelway Building Systems
Stoltz Metals
Straight Steel Sales Corporation
Strat-O-Span Buildings, Inc.
Trachte Building Systems
U.S. Metal Buildings
U.S. Prefab. Inc.
Universal Steel Structures, Inc.
Web Steel Buildings
WedgCor, Inc.
Western Steel Building Systems, LLC
Wright Building Systems
WS Steel Structures LP

*Duplicates removed

Appendix B
University of Phoenix Informed Consent

Dear ,

My name is George Rideout, and I am a student at the University of Phoenix working on a Doctor of Business Administration degree. I am conducting a research study entitled *U.S. Metal Building Industry: A Qualitative Study on Managing Change to Create a Competitive Advantage.* The purpose of the research study is to identify change management strategies used by leaders in the U.S. metal building industry.

Your participation will involve completing an anticipated three internet-based questionnaires over a maximum period of seven weeks. Each questionnaire should take no longer than 30 minutes to complete. Your participation in this study is voluntary. If you choose not to participate or to withdraw from the study at any time, you can do so without penalty or loss of benefit to yourself. The results of the research study may be published but your identity will remain confidential and your name will not be disclosed to any outside party.

In this research, there are no foreseeable risks to you: none

Although there may be no direct benefit to you, a possible benefit of your participation is the research may identify change management techniques and strategies. The techniques and strategies may benefit the U.S. metal building industry and industry in general, including the academic community.

If you have any questions concerning the research study, please call me at 404-200-4168 or e-mail me at grideout@email.phoenix.edu.

As a participant in this study, you should understand the following:

1. You may decline to participate or withdraw from participation at any time without consequences.
2. Your identity will be kept confidential.
3. George Rideout, the researcher, has thoroughly explained the parameters of the research study and all of your questions and concerns have been addressed.
4. If the interviews are recorded, you must grant permission for the researcher, George Rideout, to digitally record the interview. You understand that the information from the recorded interviews may be transcribed. The researcher will

structure a coding process to assure that anonymity of your name is protected.

5. Data will be stored in a secure and locked area. The data will be held for a period of three years, and then destroyed.

6. The research results will be used for publication.

"By signing this form you acknowledge that you understand the nature of the study, the potential risks to you as a participant, and the means by which your identity will be kept confidential. Your signature on this form also indicates that you are 18 years old or older and that you give your permission to voluntarily serve as a participant in the study described."

Signature of the interviewee _____ Date _____

Signature of the researcher _____ Date _____

Appendix C
Questionnaire

Please answer the following questions based on your knowledge and
experience in the U.S. metal building industry:

1. How do you define change management?

2. What significant change have you experienced in your organization?

3. What precipitated these significant changes?

4. How do you recognize or forecast these change forces?

5. How do you differentiate between internal and external change forces?

6. What caused internal change in your organization?

7. How did you respond to internal change?

8. What caused external change in your organization?

9. How did you respond to external change?

10. How do you perceive the internal and external change forces influence
    managing change effectively in your organization?

11. How do these change forces hinder or support your organizations ability
    to compete?

12. How do you define competitive advantage?

13. How do you believe change management may create a competitive
    advantage for your organization?

Appendix D
Coding and Thematic Process

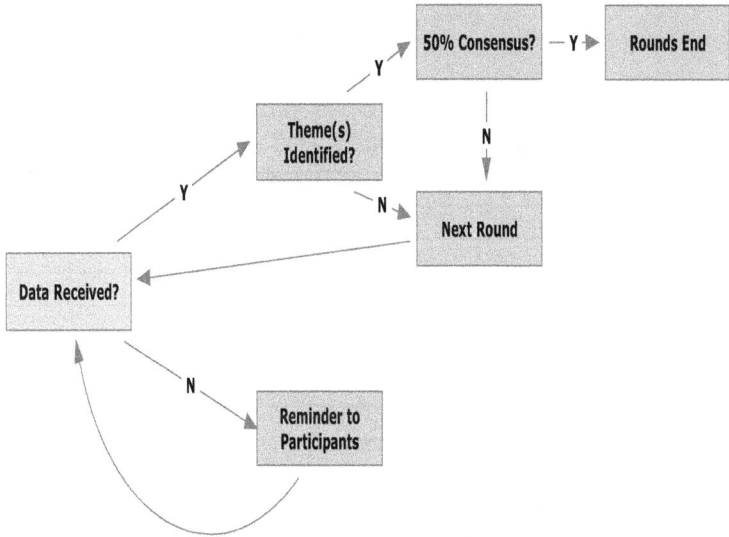

Appendix E
NVIVO9 Round One Word Query Results

Q1	Q2	Q3	Q4	Q5	Q6	Q7	Q8
Change	Change	Company	Change	Forces	Change	Change	Change
Management	Sales	Changes	Trends	External	Internal	Changes	Changes
Process	Survive	Madness	Drivers	Change	Orders	Internal	External
Changes	Approach	Market	Economy	Internal	Caused	People	Organization
Organization	Business	Money	Forecast	Caused	Changes	Better	Acting
Adapt	Experienced	Ourselves	History	Which	Customers	Driven	Administration
Define	Force	Sales	Market	Business	Increase	Involved	Again
Elements	Market	Significant	Trying	Control	Taking	Management	Agenda
Making	Opportunity	Activity	Unforeseen	Government	Which	Respond	Answer
Outside	Organization	Aligning	Again	Governments	Based	Teams	Banks
Product	System	Banks	Ahead	Impact	Better	Acceptance	Because
State	Systems	Biggest	Along	Industry	Caused	Adapted	Businesses
Through	Through	Business	Analysis	Interest	Changing	Adjustments	Buying
Within	Viewpoint	Caused	Anecdotal	Losers	Competition	Allowed	Caused
Ability	Activity	Cliff	Artificial	Manipulation	Competitive	Almost	Challenges
Actions	Actually	Companies	Available	Market	Complete	Amount	Commitments
Affect	Allow	Competes	Based	Special	Costs	Asked	Construction
Alter	American	Competitive	Beings	Winners	Economic	Buying	Create
Altered	Areas	Contracted	Building	Actions	Efficiency	Channels	Created
Being	forced	Created	Businesses	Adjust	Experienced	Commitments	Creators
Business	Around	Currently	Changes	Bailouts	External	Communication	Current
Communication	Autocad	Customer	Clear	Based	Focus	Complete	Customer
Company	Based	Customers	Close	Between	Forces	Consensus	Demand
Competition	Being	Decreased	Company	Beyond	Increases	Constantly	Don't
Conditions	Builder	Development	Complex	Building	Indicated	Cross	Economic

Q9	Q10	Q11	Q12	Q13
Customers	Change	Change	Advantage	Change
Adjusting	Forces	Compete	Customer	Organization
Change	External	Competitors	Competitive	Management
Continued	Internal	Forces	Needs	Advantage
Downturn	Managing	Other	Company	Competitive
Product	Company	Support	Targeted	Create
Accepted	Customers	Ability	Those	Economy
Additional	Effectively	Business	Defined	Improve
Advance	Failure	Changes	Every	Individuals
Allow	Influence	Competition	Supplier	Involves
Answer	Information	Customer	Anything	Right
Aware	Making	Market	Arise	Successful
Became	Needs	Solution	Broad	Teams
Broadened	Accordingly	Tried	Create	Value
Build	Actions	Where	Customers	Within
Built	Adjust	While	Define	Ability
Business	Attention	Adjust	Gives	Additionally
Closely	Based	Adjustments	Market	Affected
Competition	Basic	Advantage	Process	Allow
Completely	Become	Athletes	Satisfaction	Approach
Developed	Behind	Because	Service	Assignment
Directly	Believe	Believe	Should	Automatically
Dividends	Better	Below	Therefore	Becoming
Downturns	Blocks	Benefits	Willing	Believe
Because	Building	Bureaucratic	Ability	Better

Appendix F
Round One Questions and Responses

Q1. How do you define change management?

Participant 1: The process of leading or guiding staff through modifying processes or procedures.

Participant 2: I would define change management as management that responds to the outside elements making changes reflective of the outside elements.

Participant 3: Change management is a process that an organization or team within an organization uses to affect change or transition within the group from a current state to a desired state. This process is structured and involves the teammates in the decision making/ development process.

Participant 4: Change Management is the process of planning and executing actions that alter the direction of our company. This can be through organizational changes or new focuses on costs, new product lines, and/or new markets.

Participant 5: Recognition of the need to adapt to altered conditions in the business environment and doing so in a thought out, planned for way.

Participant 6: The ability to adapt one's style or organization to the constant changes being created by market demands, competition, product innovation, new communication systems, scarcity of resources or government interference.

Q2. What significant change have you experienced in your organization?

Participant 1: Scale down of business levels thus reducing staff and increasing individual responsibilities over multiple areas of the business.

Participant 2: We have been forced to downsize our work force and general overhead in order to survive in the current economy.

Participant 3: We have experienced a major change in our organizations sales approach. We have transitioned from a bid system where we bid any and all opportunities, to a system that does not involve public plan rooms. We develop partnerships with key customers, through frequent communication either by personal visit or phone conversations and allow our sales force to determine the viability of the sales opportunity. This approach ensures that we bid only jobs that we have a good opportunity to sell and get the "last look".

Participant 4: Our revenues decreased 30% from 2008 to 2009. We reduced headcount and actually sold a division to manage our cash and survive the "Great Recession".

Participant 5: The need to survive in a period of diminished sales revenue and declining margins due to a drastic reduction in market activity.

Participant 6: Our organization is built around dynamic change that is made possible by a highly motivated and flexible workforce. The greatest change the industry has witnessed from a distribution viewpoint is the move away from exclusivity in our builder networks. From a market viewpoint, the exporting of American manufacturing jobs based on horrible government policy has dried up our manufacturing building markets and moved forced us more into the commercial and institutional sectors. We are currently also going through a large technical change as AutoCAD detailing systems is being replaced by BIM systems.

Q3. What precipitated these significant changes?

Participant 1: Economic downturn in the economy impacting our industry.

Participant 2: We were forced to take a look at our entire organizational structure due to significant loss in sales where our overhead ratio was not proportional to our sales.

Participant 3: The madness that is currently the reality of the competitive bid market. We have realized that the company that makes the biggest mistake is the company that wins the job. We are simply trying to separate ourselves from this madness and aligning ourselves with like-minded companies.

Participant 4: The banks stopped lending money to our customer's customers, so the business levels contracted significantly. It was like falling off a cliff if you look at our order activity.

Participant 5: Turbulence in financial markets decreased the money supply for the kinds of work our company competes for.

Participant 6: Normal market changes as well as government meddling in the free enterprise process caused some of it. The BIM move has been created by the development of superior technology.

Q4. How do you recognize or forecast these change forces?

Participant 1: It is difficult to have a clear crystal ball. Obviously we use data and trends available to our market based on housing and industrial statistics along with other economic indicators.

Participant 2: We base our forecasts on word of mouth, historical data as well as current market and vendor trends.

Participant 3: Through analysis of our bid history and win history. Once again we are simply trying to use our resources in a manner that makes their efforts most effective for our company.

Participant 4: Fortunately, we saw trends in our orders and heard many concerns from our customers ahead of time. That is shy we were in a position to sell the division we sold for a reasonable price.

Participant 5: Close reading of industry newsletters, financial reports, and anecdotal information from visitors to many businesses, such as vendors and truck drivers.

Participant 6: You don't. Unforeseen change is exactly that, unforeseen. You best handle it, not by trying to forecast the changes, but by building an organization that is well prepared for change whatever it may be. From a strategic viewpoint, forecasting and planning are far less important than preparation. The variables in the economy are so varied and complex that no economist ever gets them right. What you can count on is the human beings will react in predictable ways to drivers of the economy, such as tax laws, artificial shortages, subs.

Q5. How do you differentiate between internal and external change forces?

Participant 1: External change forces have an impact on our industry and internal impact our company.

Participant 2: I look at external change forces, which then dictate internal changes. We react internally based upon the external change forces.

Participant 3: unsure that we do at this time.

Participant 4: Internal forces are caused within our organization when we ignore trends, like decreasing orders and keep spending like we did during higher volume times. External forces are market shifts and competitor's actions that we need to adjust our business to.

Participant 5: The former has a greater degree of self-control; the latter contains factors beyond our control.

Participant 6: Internal change forces are typically caused by an organizations need to compete for customers, employees and investors, all of which are needed for a business to survive. External forces are divided into two categories. The first category is caused by the normal evolution of competitors, technology, building codes etc., which tend to have a positive effect on the industry and force constant improvement. The second external driver is manipulation caused by governments and special interest groups. This can fall into special interest legislation, overtaxing, currency manipulation, etc. and puts the government in a position of trying to pick winners and losers. The market is great and picking winners and losers through fair competition and society prospers. Governments, especially our government, are horrible at this and needs to stay completely out of differential taxes, subsidies, bailouts etc. since they are all an outcome of manipulation.

Q6. What caused internal change in your organization?

Participant 1: Change in ownership and management styles.

Participant 2: Internal change is primarily based upon external change forces. We also have been involved with a complete organizational review, which indicated some needed internal changes which some were undertaken.

Participant 3: Primary reason is the changes that have occurred in the market place. We have experienced a significant economic down turn and an increase in the competitive landscape.

Participant 4: Internal change has been caused by reductions in orders as well as increases in orders. We focus on taking care of customers, so when orders drop, we need to change.

Participant 5: The need to cut costs, increase efficiency and lower prices.

Participant 6: Most of our change has been the result of pursuing success. We have gone from a very small, one plant operation to one of the largest in the industry. This has largely been caused by taking care of our customers and their changing needs better than our entrenched competition.

Q7. How did you respond to internal change?

Participant 1: Adapted to the changes by trying to understand the strengths of the changes and buying into the improvements.

Participant 2: My response to internal change was to evaluate how these changes effected my job description. I then made the adjustments, which allowed me to make better use of my time to help pick up the pieces that fell by the wayside with the changes.

Participant 3: I responded favorably, due to the fact that I was the one instituting the change. The process involved many meetings with management then other internal teammates to ensure that we had complete acceptance of the teams involved.

Participant 4: We offered early retirement, had layoffs, and asked our people to be flexible and move to where the work was.

Participant 5: Reduced staff, cross-trained individuals, opened channels of and increased the amount of communication and focused more on consensus management.

Participant 6: By hiring, gifted, driven people who naturally respond to customer needs. Every one of our people is under an incentive plan that rewards them and their teams for meeting customer commitments. Almost all internal change is driven by our people constantly looking for ways to get better.

Q8. What caused external change in your organization?

Participant 1: Again, the economic turndown had a big impact on changes within our organization.

Participant 2: External change has been primarily reaction to the poor economy.

Participant 3: unsure how to answer because most of our changes have been internal.

Participant 4: Banks not lending money and end users not buying our products and the same rate as they had been.

Participant 5: Imprudent financial oversight of national and global markets by various gov't entities.

Participant 6: Our market demand is down 50% from 2007 due largely to government manipulation. Our customer base is small to medium businesses and they are terrified of the current administration's agenda. You don't create jobs by punishing private sector job creators. Since we do not lay off employees, the construction recession has created huge challenges in meeting our commitments to our people while acting responsibly toward stockholders.

Q9. How did you respond to external change?

Participant 1: Accepted additional responsibilities and roles to handle positions eliminated due to volume downturn.

Participant 2: I became more keenly aware of our financial plight in which previously I was not directly involved. I have spent the last eighteen months closely monitoring and adjusting our financial situation to allow us to get back on our feet.

Participant 3: Unsure how to answer most of our change has been internal.

Participant 4: By adjusting our inventory levels and our pricing in the market to match the competition. We have also expanded our product line offerings.

Participant 5: Broadened our service area to include more potential customers, developed a completely new product line, revised how sell to customers.

Participant 6: Our long term philosophy has been to reserve profits from the past to build security for the future. We not only have survived the downturn but also continued investing in our business by drawing from our nest egg we had built in past years. A practice of no layoffs and continued stockholder dividends is only possible by funding downturns in advance. Unlike the government, we do not survive unless we are fiscally responsible. Because we have a nest egg, we have been able to treat our employees and our customers exactly as we would have in an upturn.

Q10. How do you perceive the internal and external change forces influence managing change effectively in your organization?

Participant 1: The internal and external change forces have a major influence on managing change in our company. Failure to manage change leaves us open to total failure. Managing the changes makes us stronger and more competitive in a down market.

Participant 2: I believe that the external and internal change forces forced me and my partner to become better managers due to these change forces.

Participant 3: Due to the relative flat nature of our management structure we are able to adjust to change in a timelier manner. I feel that we see opportunities to make improvements and act accordingly.

Participant 4: The change forces have helped us focus on what is important to our customers. We have also returned to our basic building blocks when making decisions. This time, the change happened faster than expected, so we were more reactive than we wanted to be. However, we were able to communicate the needs for our actions effectively.

Participant 5: Both require vigilant attention so that our company does not fall behind in the marketplace.

Participant 6: No change for us. Virtually all change is based on customer needs that are best initiated by the employees who have direct involvement with individual customers. In my position, I have a different pool of information than most of my teammates, so my job is best done by sharing strategic information with them and letting them incorporate that input into their decision making and recommendations.

Q11. How do these change forces hinder or support your organization's ability to compete?

Participant 1: External forces from competition can create hardships when competing in markets where one or more of our competitors have tried to "buy" business by selling at or below market costs. This creates opportunity for tough decisions when looking at potential projects.

Participant 2: I believe due to our company size we are able to compete in a segment of our marketplace due to the change forces where other competitors cannot.

Participant 3: They support because we are able to react quickly when adjustments in our methods or philosophy are needed.

Participant 4: The competitive nature of our business has caused significant margin erosion over the past 2 years. We have been effective when our customers understand that our value proposition focuses on a lower cost for the total solution. We are not the low cost producer of our products. However, by combining great customer service and other tangible benefits, we are part of a low cost solution.

Participant 5: Our changes are done only to support our ability to compete.

Participant 6: Our dynamics give us a huge advantage in rapidly changing times. While other companies are trying to forecast change and develop management responses as part of a bureaucratic process, we are like professional athletes who immediately adjust to changes in competition, playing conditions, rules etc. We saw our market share increase 40% last year as our competitors tried to respond to change while we were responding to customer needs.

Q12. How do you define competitive advantage?

Participant 1: For us we feel our competitive advantage is our name recognition along with our customer service.

Participant 2: Competitive advantage generally is defined as a cost advantage over a competitor. I feel that a competitive advantage can be anything that gives your Company a leg up on the competition. It can be location, response time. It can be almost anything that gives you "The advantage."

Participant 3: Competitive advantage can best be defined as flexibility. The ability to be flexible when the market changes, to be able to listen to the market and then react to what it is telling you. The key to this is listening to your customers and then developing and implementing an action plan to address the opportunities as they arise.

Participant 4: Competitive advantage is what we do better than any one we compete with. Our quality and customer service is a competitive advantage for us.

Participant 5: Having a natural (such as closeness to a customer and therefore lower freight cost) or developed (such as a different and more efficient process or product) factor that provides a compelling reason to customers to purchase our goods.

Participant 6: To me, competitive advantage is achieved in a five-step process:

1. **Define Targeted Needs**—First, a company must create a differentiation that allows them to uniquely meet the needs of a target customer base. Commercial success requires that the needs (products, services or both) not only be targeted, but also that the customer places high value on the satisfaction of those needs and is therefore willing to pay for that satisfaction.
2. **Meet Those Needs Consistently**—Second, the company must excel operationally at predictably meeting the defined needs of that customer base.
3. **Stand up to customer evaluation**—Third, the customer, not the company, must judge that the supplier has indeed met those unique needs and would have strong desire to buy from that supplier in the future.
4. **Achieve Word of Mouth Endorsement**—Fourth, every customer should be, not willing but anxious, to recommend the supplier to other people within his/her network.
5. **Create broad based awareness**—Last, the company, through targeted communication strategies, must get the word out to a broad

population base, such that every customer in the targeted demography, geography, etc. with like addressed needs is aware of the company and is likely to consider the company when those needs arise. Simply put our goal is that every customer who we want to sell to should want to buy from us. That is the definition of competitive advantage!!!

Q13. How do you believe change management may create a competitive advantage for your organization?

Participant 1: This is happening as we work to manage change by becoming leaner and focusing on the right markets. It has required us to strengthen our team and improve our communications internally and externally.

Participant 2: As the economy comes back we are positioned to better respond to the marketplace where many of our competitors have been forced to cut back so much that it will take some time to bring them back to service levels of a normal economy.

Participant 3: Change management by its definition is a structured approach that involves the different individuals and teams within an organization. Additionally change management involves systematic diagnosis of an organization's need and ability to change. Considering these statements, by involving the individuals and affected teams within our organization we get the best input from the people who are in the trenches to ensure we develop the best plan for change.

Participant 4: It will not create a new competitive advantage for us, but is has and will allow us to improve our system and increase our competitive advantage. We know that our business model is successful, and change management will help us move forward in that successful direction faster.

Participant 5: Provides an orderly response to internal and external stimuli, which prevents knee jerk panic and loss of efficiency and morale.

Participant 6: As stated earlier, our organization automatically changes as the needs of customers change due to the dynamics of our incentive systems. Every employee is treated as an entrepreneurial value generator. If you hire gifted employees, put them in the right assignment and reward them for creating value as a team; they will dynamically change as market demands change.

Appendix G
Round Two Questions and Responses

Q1. How do you define change management?

The following definition is based on participant round one survey responses. Please answer yes or no if you agree with the definition, and note any recommended changes or comments in the corresponding text box.

Change management is a dynamically structured team process of planning and execution, in which, leaders recognize change, and adapt the organization to meet altered conditions in the business environment, created by forces such as competition, technology, and scarcity of resources.

1. Yes – 83% (5 of 6)

2. No - 0%

3. Recommended changes or additions – 17% (1 of 6)

Q2. What significant change have you experienced in your organization?

Please select from the following. You may select more than one answer. If all apply please check the appropriate box. Please enter any additional comments or changes in the text box.

1. Significantly reduced revenue and margins – 100% (6 of 6)

2. Downsizing such as headcount and expenses – 83% (5 of 6)

3. Increased workloads on fewer employees – 83% (5 of 6)

4. Modifying business strategy, such as how the organization markets products and services to reduce expenses and operating costs – 33% (2 of 6)

5. Technological changes to enhance organizational competitive advantage – 50% (3 of 6)

6. All of the above – 17% (1 of 6) **included in above

7. Recommended changes or additions – 17% (1 of 6)

Q3. What precipitated these significant changes?

Please select from the following. You may select more than one answer. If all apply please check the appropriate box. Please enter any additional comments or changes in the text box.

1. Economic environment – 100% (6 of 6)

2. Increasingly competitive bid market – 66% (4 of 6)

3. Bank lending practices and financial market instability – 66% (4 of 6)

4. Government policies – 33% (2 of 6)

5. Technological advances – 17% (1 of 6)

6. All of the above – 0%

7. Recommended changes or additions – 33% (2 of 6)

Q4. How do you recognize or forecast these change forces?

Please select from the following. You may select more than one answer. If all apply please check the appropriate box. Please enter any additional comments or changes in the text box.

1. Word of mouth, i.e. suppliers, customers – 100% (6 of 6)

2. Economic indicators such as housing and industrial statistics – 50% (3 of 6)G

3. Historical data and trends – 33% (2 of 6)

4. Customer buying behaviors and concerns – 83% (5 of 6)

5. Promote organizational preparedness to meet changing market conditions – 33% (2 of 6)

6. All of the above – 17% (1 of 6) **included in above

7. Recommended changes or additions – 33% (2 of 6)

Q5. How do you differentiate between internal and external change forces?

Please select from the following. You may select more than one answer. If all apply please check the appropriate box. Please enter any additional comments or changes in the text box.

1. External change influences the industry, and internal change affects only the organization – 66% (4 of 6)

2. External change creates the need for internal change – 66% (4 of 6)

3. External change produces events beyond the control of the organization, and internal change creates events the organization may control – 66% (4 of 6)

4. Internal change is a result of the need for the organization to compete for customers, employees, and investors; external change results from the natural evolution of competitors, technology, and changing market conditions including government intervention – 66% (4 of 6)

5. All of the above – 50% (3 of 6) **included in above

6. Recommended changes or additions – 17% (1 of 6)

Q6. What caused internal change in your organization?

Please select from the following. You may select more than one answer. If all apply please check the appropriate box. Please enter any additional comments or changes in the text box.

1. Ownership change – 17% (1 of 6)

2. Need to modify strategies because of organizational review – 33% (2 of 6)

3. Growth opportunities – 17% (1 of 6)

4. Reduced sales volume – 83% (5 of 6)

5. Heightened competitive environment – 83% (5 of 6)

6. Response to external economic conditions to reduce expenses and increase efficiency – 83% (5 of 6)

7. All of the above – 0%

8. Recommended changes or additions – 17% (1 of 6)

Q7. How did you respond to internal change?

Please select from the following. You may select more than one answer. If all apply please check the appropriate box. Please enter any additional comments or changes in the text box.

1. Adapted by trying to understand the strengths of the change(s) and buying into the improvements – 33% (2 of 6)

2. Evaluated changes and made necessary organizational adjustments – 83% (5 of 6)

3. Ensured team synergy and buy-in – 33% (2 of 6)

4. Increased communication in organization – 66% (4 of 6)

5. Developed consensus style management – 33% (2 of 6)

6. Made hard decisions such as reducing overhead and operating expenses including employee layoffs – 50% (3 of 6)

7. Accepted change and looked for ways to maximize organizational benefit – 66% (4 of 6)

8. All of the above – 17% (1 of 6) **included in above

9. Recommended changes or additions – 17% (1 of 6)

Q8. What caused external change in your organization?

Please select from the following. You may select more than one answer. If all apply please check the appropriate box. Please enter any additional comments or changes in the text box.

1. Economic environment – 83% (5 of 6)

2. Bank lending practices – 50% (3 of 6)

3. Government policies – 33% (2 of 6)

4. Heightened competitive environment – 50% (3 of 6)

5. Changing customer buying patterns and behaviors – 66% (4 of 6)

6. All of the above – 0%

7. Recommended changes or additions – 33% (2 of 6)

Q9. How did you respond to external change?

Please select from the following. You may select more than one answer. If all apply please check the appropriate box. Please enter any additional comments or changes in the text box.

1. Increased workload and responsibilities across all departments – 66% (4 of 6)

2. Increased personal involvement in daily operations including financial management – 66% (4 of 6)

3. Identified ways to reduce operating expenses including inventory levels and pricing – 83% (5 of 6)

4. Identified new product and service areas to increase potential customer base and organizational advantage – 100% (6 of 6)

5. Continued investing in the organization and its people – 50% (3 of 6)

6. Reaffirmed that preparedness and planning ahead is the best strategy for maintaining long-term organizational viability and competitive advantage – 50% (3 of 6)

7. All of the above – 33% (2 of 6) **included in above

8. Recommended changes or additions – 17% (1 of 6)

Q10. How do you perceive the internal and external change forces influence managing change effectively in your organization?

Please select from the following. You may select more than one answer. Please enter any additional comments or changes in the text box.

1. Major influence because not managing these change forces leaves organization open to failure – 50% (3 of 6)

2. Managing the changes makes us stronger and more competitive in a down market – 66% (4 of 6)

3. Managing change requires a less complex organizational structure allowing leaders to adjust quickly and take advantage of opportunities – 17% (1 of 6)

4. The change forces help the organization become more focused on customer needs – 50% (3 of 6)

5. The change forces increase leader awareness and force leader effectiveness – 33% (2 of 6)

6. The change forces create awareness that a proactive rather than reactive management style is best – 17% (1 of 6)

7. Little influence because my organization already seeks out change and adapts to customer needs – 17% (1 of 6)

8. Recommended changes or additions – 17% (1 of 6)

Q11. How do these change forces hinder or support your organizations ability to compete?

Please select from the following. You may select more than one answer. If all apply please check the appropriate box. Please enter any additional comments or changes in the text box.

1. All changes in the organization focus on enhancing ability to compete – 33% (2 of 6)

2. The change forces create a competitive advantage because our organization is constantly adapting to meet customer needs rather than reacting to change like many of our less prepared competitors – 50% (3 of 6)

3. Company size allows our organization to take advantage of rapidly changing markets faster than our competitors – 50% (3 of 6)

4. The change forces create a heightened awareness of organizational capabilities and value-added services for customers – 50% (3 of 6)

5. The change forces sometimes create hardships and tough decisions because of increasingly competitive markets and scarce resources – 33% (2 of 6)

6. All of the above – 17% (1 of 6)

7. Recommended changes or additions – 0%

Q12. How do you define competitive advantage?

The following definition is based on participant round one survey responses. Please answer yes or no if you agree with the definition, and note any recommended changes or comments in the corresponding text box.

A competitive advantage means flexibility, customer loyalty, and performing better than competitors. The organization will achieve a competitive advantage by reacting and adapting faster, listening to customer needs better, and developing strategies to differentiate it and compel customers to buy, recommend, and place a premium value on its products and services.

    1.   Yes – 66% (4 of 6)

    2.   No – 0%

    3.   Recommended changes or additions – 33% (2 of 6)

Q13. How do you believe change management may create a competitive advantage for your organization?

Please select from the following. You may select more than one answer. If all apply please check the appropriate box. Please enter any additional comments or changes in the text box.

    1.   Increases focus and awareness of operating environment – 50% (3 of 6)

    2.   Increases communication in organization – 66% (4 of 6)

    3.   Promotes team philosophy – 66% (4 of 6)

    4.   Promotes operational efficiency, and helps identify ways to work smarter with less resources – 33% (2 of 6)

    5.   Promotes systematic diagnosis of organizational needs and ability to change – 17% (1 of 6)

    6.   Will enhance existing organizational competitive advantage(s) by demanding constant improvement – 66% (4 of 6)

    7.   Lessens the knee jerk response and enhances efficiency and employee morale during times of change – 33% (2 of 6)

    8.   Supports the call for dynamic organizations who constantly adapt to customer and stakeholder needs, and reward employees for

creating value in the organization – 66% (4 of 6)

9. All of the above – 17% (1 of 6)

10. Recommended changes or additions – 0%

Q14. Please identify, in your opinion, the three greatest change forces facing the U.S. metal building industry in the next five to ten years.

Q15. Please identify, in your opinion, the three greatest change forces facing the U.S. metal building industry in the next 25 years.

Appendix H
Round Three Questions and Responses

Q1. How do you recognize or forecast these change forces?

Please select one answer from the following. You may select only one box.

1. Economic indicators such as housing and industrial statistics (50%) – 50% (2 of 4)

2. Historical data and trends (33%) – 25% (1 of 4)

3. Promote organizational preparedness to meet changing market conditions (33%) – 0%

4. Steel prices versus substitution material prices (17%) – 0%

5. Monitor government policies and legislation (17%) – 25% (1 of 4)

Q2. What caused external change in your organization?

Please select one answer from the following. You may select only one box.

1. Bank lending practices (50%) – 25% (1 of 4)

2. Government policies (33%) – 25% (1 of 4)

3. Heightened competitive environment (50%) – 50% (2 of 4)

4. Raw material prices (17%) – 0%

Q3. How do you perceive the internal and external change forces influence managing change effectively in your organization?

Please select two answers from the following. You may only select two boxes.

1. Major influence, because not managing these change forces leaves organization open to failure (50%) – 50% (2 of 4)

2. Managing change requires a less complex organizational structure allowing leaders to adjust quickly and take advantage of opportunities (17%) – 25% (1 of 4)

3. The change forces help the organization become more focused

on customer needs (50%) – 75% (3 of 4)

4. The change forces increase leader awareness and force leader effectiveness (33%) – 0%

5. The change forces create awareness that a proactive rather than reactive management style is best (17%) – 25% (1 of 4)

6. Little influence because my organization already seeks out change and adapts to customer needs (17%) – 25% (1 of 4)

Q4. How do these change forces hinder or support your organizations ability to compete?

Please select three answers from the following. You may only select three boxes.

1. All changes in the organization focus on enhancing ability to compete (33%) – 50% (2 of 4)

2. The change forces create a competitive advantage because our organization is constantly adapting to meet customer needs rather than reacting to change like many of our less prepared competitors (50%) – 75% (3 of 4)

3. Company size allows our organization to take advantage of rapidly changing markets faster than our competitors (50%) – 100% (4 of 4)

4. The change forces create a heightened awareness of organizational capabilities and value-added services for customers (50%) – 75% (3 of 4)

5. The change forces sometimes create hardships and tough decisions because of increasingly competitive markets and scarce resources (33%) – 0%

Q5. Please select the top three change forces facing the U.S. metal building industry in the next five to ten years.

Please select no more than three answers.

1. Availability of capital – 50% (2 of 4)

2. Availability of skilled labor – 0%

3. Energy codes – 75% (3 of 4)

4. Government policies including market manipulation, and tax laws – 75% (3 of 4)

5. Industry consolidation – 0%

6. Rapidly changing steel market – 25% (1 of 6)

7. Raw material costs versus alternatives – 25% (1 of 6)

8. Rebirth of competitive bid market and the lack of negotiated work – 25% (1 of 6)

9. Unstable domestic economy – 25% (1 of 6)

10. Varied building design evident throughout industry – 0%

Q6. Please select the top three change forces facing the U.S. metal building industry in the next 25 years.

Please select no more than three answers.

1. Availability of capital – 0%

2. Availability of skilled labor because of retiring labor force – 33% (1 of 3)

3. Energy codes – 33% (1 of 3)

4. Foreign competition – 33% (1 of 3)

5. Government policies including market manipulation, regulations, and tax laws – 67% (2 of 3)

6. Industry consolidation - beyond U.S. – 0%

7. Increase in alternative construction methods and products – 33% (1 of 3)

8. New technology – 33% (1 of 3)

9. Rapidly changing steel market – 0%

10. Raw material costs versus alternatives – 33% (1 of 3)

11. Rebirth of competitive bid market and the lack of negotiated work – 0%

12. Shrinking consumer base because of baby boomer retirement – 0%

13. Unstable domestic economy – 33% (1 of 3)

14. Varied building design evident throughout industry – 0%

Appendix I
Final Consensus Data

Q1. How do you define change management?

Yes - 83% (5 out of 6) – **

Change management is a dynamically structured team process of planning and execution in which leaders recognize change and adapt the organization to meet altered conditions in the business environment, created by forces such as competition, product innovation, and scarcity of resources.

Q2. What significant change have you experienced in your organization?

    A.   Significantly reduced revenue and margins - 100% (6 of 6) – **

    B.   Downsizing such as headcount and expenses - 83% (5 of 6) – **

    C.   Increased workloads on fewer employees - 83% (5 of 6) – **

Q3. What precipitated these changes?

    A.   General economic environment - 100% (6 of 6) – **

    B.   Increasingly competitive bid market - 66% (4 of 6) – **

    C.   Bank lending practices and financial market instability - 66% (4 of 6) – **

Q4. How do you recognize or forecast these change forces?

    A.   Word of mouth, i.e. suppliers, customers - 100% (6 of 6) - **

    B.   Economic indicators such as housing and industrial statistics - 50% (2 of 4) - ***

    D.   Customer buying behaviors and concerns - 83% (5 of 6) – **

Q5. How do you differentiate between internal and external change forces?

    A. External change influences the industry, and internal change affects only the organization – 66% (4 of 6) - **

    B. External change creates the need for internal change – 66% (4 of 6) - **

    C. External change produces events beyond the control of the organization; internal change creates events the organization may control – 66% (4 of 6) - **

    D. Internal change is a result of the need for the organization to compete for customers, employees, and investors; external change results from the natural evolution of competitors, technology, and changing market conditions including government intervention - 66% (4 of 6) - **

Q6. What caused internal change in your organization?

    D. Reduced sales volume - 83% (5 of 6) - **

    E. Heightened competitive environment - 83% (5 of 6) - **

    F. Response to external economic conditions to reduce expenses and increase efficiency - 83% (5 of 6) - **

Q7. How did you respond to internal change?

B – Evaluated changes and made necessary organizational adjustments - 83% (5 of 6) - **

D – Increased communication in organization - 66% (4 of 6) - **

G – Accepted change and looked for ways to maximize organizational benefit - 66% (4 of 6) - **

Q8. What caused external change in your organization?

A – Economic environment - 83% (5 of 6) - **

D – Heightened competitive environment - 50% (2 of 4) - ***

E – Changing customer buying patterns and behaviors - 66% (4 of 6) – **

Q9. How did you respond to external change?

A – Increased workload and responsibilities across all departments - 66% (4 of 6) - **

B – Increased personal involvement in daily operations including financial management - 66% (4 of 6) - **

C – Identified ways to reduce operating expenses including inventory levels and pricing - 83% (5 of 6) - **

D – Identified new product and service areas to increase potential customer base and organizational advantage - 66% (4 of 6) - **

Q10. How do you perceive the internal and external change forces influence managing change effectively in your organization?

A – Major influence because not managing the influences leaves organization open to failure - 50% (2 of 4) - ***

B – Managing the changes makes us stronger and more competitive in a down market - 66% (4 of 6) - **

E – The change forces help the organization become more focused on customer needs - 75% (3 of 4) – ***

Q11. How do these change forces hinder or support your organizations ability to compete?

B – The change forces create a competitive advantage because our organization is constantly adapting to meet customer needs rather than reacting to change like many of our less prepared competitors - 75% (3 of 4) - ***

C – Company size allows our organization to take advantage of rapidly changing markets faster than our competitors - 100% (4 of 4) - ***

D – The change forces create a heightened awareness of organizational capabilities and value-added services for our customers - 75% (3 of 4) – ***

Q12. How do you define competitive advantage?

Yes = 66% (4 of 6) - **

A competitive advantage means flexibility, customer loyalty, and performing better than competitors. The organization will achieve a competitive advantage by reacting and adapting faster, listening to customer needs better and developing strategies to differentiate and compel customers to buy, recommend, and place a premium value on its products and services.

Q13. How do you believe change management may create a competitive advantage for your organization?

B. Increases communication in organization – 66% (4 of 6) - **

C. Promotes team philosophy – 66% (4 of 6) - **

F. Will enhance existing organizational competitive advantage(s) by demanding constant improvement – 66% (4 of 6) - **

H. Supports the call for dynamic organizations that constantly adapt to customer and stakeholder needs, and reward employees for creating value in the organization - 66% (4 of 6) - **

Q14. Please identify in your opinion, the three greatest change forces facing the U.S. metal building industry in the next five to 10 years.

A. Availability of capital - 50% (2 of 4) - ***

C. Energy codes - 75% (3 of 4) - ***

D. Government policies including market manipulation, and tax laws - 75% (3 of 4) - ***

Q15. Please identify in your opinion, the three greatest change forces facing the U.S. metal building industry in the next 25 years.

E. Government policies including market manipulation, regulations, and tax laws - 66% (2 of 3) – ***

**Round two identified consensus

***Round three identified consensus

About the Author

George W. Rideout, D.B.A., holds an MBA and numerous professional certifications including the certified six sigma black belt (CSSBB) and the FCIB international certified credit executive (ICCE). He has more than 16 years' experience in sales and management, leading sales teams in the United States and Canada. Dr. Rideout is a member of various professional associations including the Association of Leadership Educators (ALE), the Institute of Management Consultants (IMC), and the International Leadership Association (ILA). His research interests include change leadership, decision making, leadership studies, multiple intelligences, and systems theories.

product-compliance

913